THE ROYALTY OF LEAR

Arthur G. Davis

Assistant Professor of English

St. John's University
New York

Published by the

St. John's University Press

Copyright 1974 © St. John's University, New York

Library of Congress Cataloging in Publication Data

Davis, Arthur G. The Royalty of Lear – Includes bibliographical references.
1. Shakespeare, William, 1564-1616. King Lear. I. Title.
PR2819.D38   822.3'3   74-7115   ISBN 0-87075-073-9

Dedication:

To Arthur Junior,
Paul and Giselle

PREFACE

King Lear has often been called the greatest of Shakespeare's plays. The subject is a mighty one which transcends easy analysis. Even the opening scene is difficult to sum up adequately; it must be treated in detail with the most careful attention to the human psychology of those who take an active part in it, the poetry of this climactic moment in the life of Lear, and even the probable thoughts of those who stand to one side or the other and merely witness what takes place.

The basic realities with which Shakespeare deals in this play must be viewed as existing in and of themselves. They do not become impressive by being dressed in great poetry. Rather it is great poetry which alone can express their full meaning. Nor do they become obvious in the hands of a lesser writer; they simply escape him. "What Shakespeare has done with his material" is a meaningless approach unless the material itself is true (in the most deeply philosophical sense of the word) and the dramatist is seen, not as a creator, but as an interpreter.

To say that something is true does not mean that it cannot be construed differently according to one view or another. Neither does it mean that all views are equally valid, supposedly representing the various angles from which we all see the same thing. What it does mean, first and foremost, is a deep-seated kind of actuality that has its effect upon all with whom it comes in contact.

In approaching this question we all strive for an open mind. Convictions, however, need not be set aside but merely held in abeyance, if only long enough to see for a few short moments whatever logic may be offered in

contrary views — just as in certain branches of mathe-
matics we make assumptions we know to be false in order
to undertake the task of proving them so. In much that I
have read on *King Lear* I have detected (often the writer
makes it quite clear) that one's views of the play are his
views of life itself. Whether I agree with them or not,
there is a certain consistency that I believe proves my
initial point: the powerful appeal of the play lies
primarily in its faithfulness to life as we ourselves have
experienced it.

Of all the tragedies, *King Lear* is perhaps pre-eminent
in its concern with those deeper meanings about which
everyone has some notion, and in its limitless probing,
almost beyond our power to fathom, their inexhaustible
and manifold import. He who would interpret this play is,
I believe, facing a tremendous challenge. Were he poet and
philosopher as well as Shakespearean scholar, a book on
Lear would be the greatest test of his powers.

I confess, therefore, to a feeling of trepidation in
making the attempt. I do not write on *Lear* because I feel
adequate but because of an almost mystical call to say all
I can in the best way I know how, and I am additionally
realistic enough to know that if I can exceed myself and
write a good book, it will be little enough. Either we
approach *King Lear* with humility, or we had better go
elsewhere. This is not said in the hope of forestalling
criticism. I am not hesitant about expressing myself
directly or even with assurance. It is not so much a fear of
being wrong, a possibility that every commentator must
be willing to face, but rather the paltriness of what I may
offer as compared with the great work itself. To see the
play correctly is, of course, the beginning. But to go
beyond what we see correctly is like peering into depths
that have no bottom but are nevertheless distinct with a
jeweled visibility. To see them from one perspective is
not to deny that they may be — *must* be — viewed from

other perspectives as well, in order that something of the scope and penetration of the play itself be revealed.

The particular aspect I have chosen has been all too frequently overlooked: the royalty of Lear. In literary interpretation when one view is missing the result is likely to be, not incompleteness, but misinterpretation. What happens in the play has often been assessed as "out of proportion" to the causes. In seeking some explanation for this disproportion, many have come up with ingenious theories relating to Lear's past, including of course the kind of king he has been, as well as the earlier life of his three daughters and of other major characters. This sort of speculation is perfectly valid, provided we do not detach ourselves from the play proper to seek something that appears to be missing. Such a theory, for instance, as Lear's incestuous attraction to Goneril, which Cordelia senses intuitively or through direct knowledge, and which consequently throws a very sordid atmosphere over the "love test" in the opening scene, is a case in point.[1] It will explain much once it is improvised. Like many other theories, however, it is based on the assumption that the behavior of Lear and Cordelia is inexplicable, and we must therefore pluck something out of the dark to provide the answer. Whether Goneril was an exceedingly attractive woman who induced unnatural desires on the part of her father, I do not really know. Her beauty can be assumed as likely enough. Whether it inspired anything more in Lear than paternal pride is pure conjecture.

This particular theory would seem to have no connection with the "royalty" of Lear, unless my position be that royal persons are immune from incest. Indeed there *is* no connection. I cite the case merely to show that when we overlook certain facts and manufacture others to take their place, our notions of the protagonist and the entire play will change drastically. What I believe to be the correct view is not necessarily a refutation, in the sense that it is diametrically opposed, but rather a stressing of the very thing we imagined all along to be lacking.

Precisely what I mean by the "royalty" of Lear will become plain as I proceed. I prefer to get at the meaning gradually rather than lay down definitions — which would only have to be explained and defended anyway — at the beginning.

TABLE OF CONTENTS

I

LEAR AS KING

Similar to the classic concept of Fortune's Wheel, that only he in a high place can take a great fall, is the even more plausible concept that only the crash of something momentous can bring about momentous results. The disorder that occurs in *King Lear* is not an underlying chaos upon which has been stamped a false semblance of order, as many scholars would have us believe, presuming chaos to be the ultimate truth under all the empty forms and rituals of civilization. Rather the spreading anarchy is itself caused by the toppling of something that is mighty. What I mean by *mighty* is only partially realized in political power. The authority that Lear wields is certainly part of it, but, as the play amply demonstrates when he no longer possesses that authority, much more is involved than the mere power to command and be obeyed.

Few characters in fiction symbolize royalty as I conceive Lear to symbolize it in the opening scene of the play, in the grandeur of his patriarchal person and in every hint we have, here and later, as to the kind of ruler he has been. The fall of such a man is a great one. The results are equally so, but it is from the results that we thread our way back to what has fallen and perceive more clearly what it truly signifies. To all this we are far from blind in the beginning, but our appreciation of its full meaning is much more profound when we have lived through everything that comes of its ruination, right down to that tragic calm at the end after death has stilled the voices and the struggles of so many.

Lamb's well known comment on the staging of the play has some bearing, I think, upon much that has been written on Lear:

> So to see Lear acted, — to see an old man tottering about the stage with a walking-stick, turned out of doors by his daughters in a rainy night, has nothing in it but what is painful and disgusting. . . . On the stage we see nothing but corporal infirmities and weakness, the impotence of rage; while we read it, we see not Lear, but we are Lear, — we are in his mind, we are sustained by a grandeur which baffles the malice of daughters and storms; in the aberrations of his reason, we discover a mighty irregular power of reasoning, immethodised from the ordinary purposes of life, but exerting its powers, as the wind blows where it listeth, at will upon the corruptions and abuses of mankind.[2]

Lamb's main point, that the play cannot be adequately staged, rests on the shaky evidence of the performances he had seen in the theatre of his own day, and is certainly open to question. But he is right in denouncing the tottering old man with the walking stick as a thoroughly incongruous figure in the Miltonic power of the play itself. Stage portrayals are nothing more nor less than interpretations of character. The king we come to visualize from reading the text cannot possibly be portrayed as a pitiful old man, any more than he can be depicted according to other interpretations, equally disparaging, which Lamb would also have condemned as "painful and disgusting."

Setting aside for the moment the question of Lear's responsibility for his own downfall, we must bear in mind two important considerations. First, indisputable evidence exists within the play that Lear has been something much more than an intemperate and dictatorial king who demands to be flattered, contrary to the findings of many scholars who read his character exclusively from the "love test." Second, the vigorous drama of the middle section is possible, *only* if he has been the kind of king that his subjects have good cause to respect — to the point of reverence.

This is the Lear whom the outspoken Kent addresses, even while disputing his sentence:

> Royal Lear,
> Whom I have ever honored as my King,
> Loved as my father, as my master followed,
> As my great patron thought on in my prayers —

The devotion of Cordelia, while some may insist that Lear has forfeited his right to it, is certainly inspired by something more than a peremptory and egotistical father. She ever loves him and is moved to tears at what eventually happens to him; a deep and warm affection lies within her, not a cold sense of duty to an unworthy parent. As we shall see, even her refusal to flatter him in the first scene is not due to any paternal failure on his part. Her love, let it be granted, does more credit to her than to him, but we may concede this point without minimizing Lear or exaggerating Cordelia's devotion into something given for nothing.

The loyalty of Gloucester is constant even in the face of threats against his life:

> Though I die for it, as no less is threatened me, the King
> my old master must be relieved.

Edgar, filled with the injustice of his own sufferings, weeps at seeing Lear undergoing a fate similar to his own:

> My tears begin to take his part so much
> They'll mar my counterfeiting.

Still later, Albany speaks of the King :

A father, and a gracious aged man
Whose reverence even the head-lugged bear would lick. . .

It is no rotten authority that we see both reverenced and disreverenced, no kingship sagging under the weight of its own imbecility, no title that commands a greater respect than the man who possesses it. This last is the case with Richard II. But Lear is himself the authority that commands respect. After his downfall, all those who condemn the action are inspired by a devotion to the *man himself* . There is no discussion of legality in an abstract sense, as there is in *Richard II, Henry IV* and *Henry VI.* — There are, to be sure, personal sympathies and enmities in these other plays, but invariably under the countenance, affected or otherwise, of *legality*. Most of the discussion relating to the overthrow of Richard II and Henry VI is political in nature. In *King Lear* there is none. The person of Lear himself stands pre-eminent.

Nor is it a primitive society over which he has ruled. There are sufficient references to jurists and criminals to suggest an elaborate system of law, and the allusions to marriage vows and family love are hardly those of an ignorant people guided by tribal taboos deeply ingrained. Lear, for all the pagan past to which he supposedly belongs, is king in a sophisticated and enlightened age. Gloucester's fear that "we have seen the best of our time" carries an intimation of that apex, often seen in the history of highly civilized nations, at which an overripeness of culture brings about a certain putrefaction that may lead to disintegration and downfall. His fears may be exaggerated — the rest of the play will tell — but they would be impossible in a primitive society. Clearly the Britain of this play is a nation of considerable erudition, whatever the historical Britain may have been. Lear is not the object of some superstitious veneration on the part of a simpleminded people, nor the caretaker of a debased one. Greed, deceit, animalism exist, it is true, but so do generosity, truth and that moral idealism which speaks out freely even to the face of authority itself, and these latter are all loyal to the King.

Such is the realm over which Lear has long presided. Only as the events begin to unfold do we become acquainted with it, but our growing familiarity with the protagonist and the times in which he lives is one of development rather than contradiction. What we learn in later scenes must in some way accord with the beginning. It is on this point, understandably, that a matter of dramatic principle has caused some confusion.

No one will dispute the point that initial appearances are important in Shakespeare. Our first impression of a character is likely to be a lasting one. This is particularly true when the initial appearance is highly dramatic (which can certainly be said of Lear's performance in the opening scene) and involves actions or decisions which determine what direction the plot will now take. Not only do we attach significance to the scene at the time that it takes place, but we remember it with increasing emphasis as the terrible consequences begin to ensue. The division of the kingdom. The disowning of Cordelia. Were not these acts the cause of it all? Both in an interpretive sense, therefore, and in point of plot development, the beginning would seem to lay the foundations for all that follows. As we witness the play in its chronological order, we get a powerful impression of the wrongheadedness of Lear at the very beginning and we are so constantly reminded of it that we cannot regard it as some momentary fit of temper soon to be forgotten.

This principle — powerful first impression plus important dramatic results — certainly has validity, and I am not suggesting for a moment that it does not apply to

King Lear. It does. The precise way in which we interpret it, however, is the point in dispute, and not whether we follow it or ignore it. The wrongheadedness of Lear, or whatever term by which we choose to designaté it, is established beyond dispute. Now, how much or how little or exactly what does it tell us about Lear? Paying the strictest attention to the man himself, the characters most closely involved in what he does and the particular circumstances of the opening scene, let us read all "with modesty enough and likelihood to lead it."

What I might call the case against Lear rests on two facts, both taking place in the scene we are considering: The division of the kingdom and the love test — or at least the manner in which Lear conducts the love test. So much needs to be said about each that I will defer the second of these to the next chapter, begging the reader to keep in mind everything that I say in this one. The division of the kingdom and the love test are so closely intertwined that it is impossible to consider one without the other.

Much has been written about the foolishness of dividing the kingdom. But we must be careful to distinguish between Lear's original plan and the one he hastily seizes upon as a result of his falling out with Cordelia. The whole question of Lear's conduct bears very much on what he carefully plans and what he does in a moment of fierce passion. Henry V. Jaffa[3] has written a convincing defense of the original plan, showing it to be worked out with the greatest care. Jaffa's principal points are that Lear would occupy the central and richest third of the kingdom and keep the dukes separated, at the same time securing the adhesion of the lords of these outlying districts through marriage with the royal house. Cordelia's marriage to Burgundy, which Jaffa says Lear preferred, would give the King a strong ally on the Continent who is a rival to France, Britain's traditional enemy. The essay demonstrates quite clearly, I think, that the plan was a wise one which took all eventualities into consideration. Furthermore, there is no evidence that anyone in the play ever thought the plan a foolish one. At the very beginning of the play Gloucester and Kent are discussing the division as originally conceived. Though Kent is out-spoken whenever the occasion demands and Gloucester — a little more discreet than Kent — comments frequently on whatever he feels to be wrong, neither of them says a word in criticism of the King's project. The Fool, who is so voluble about the folly of permitting the daughters to rule the father, does not appear in the play until after the substitute plan has been acted upon, and indeed has actually begun to have results. All the Fool's comments are about the second plan, not the first.

As Bramson[4] points out, dividing a kingdom would not of itself be improbable, since Elizabethans would remember the abdication of Charles V, and Charlemagne did actually divide his kingdom into three among his children. Lear's daughters, if they are to be his heirs, will sooner or later inherit the kingdom, whether by his death or by some such plan as he has already devised. We may have our reasons for thinking the plan a mistake, but we must consider what possible alternative the King had and what the results might have been if he had acted upon it. The division of the kingdom could be avoided by having the eldest, Goneril, the sole inheritor. Lear will not live forever, and it boots little whether the decision to split the kingdom or keep it whole be made now or postponed to a later date. If the kingdom is to remain intact, however, it must be passed on to one daughter only, and it is difficult to see how Lear could select the youngest — who, as events would seem to demonstrate, will prove to be the one most fit to rule — without dispossessing the other two, and thereby setting conditions for the "future strife" which he wants to prevent now. Goneril is the only likely choice for sole rule, though this would be less satisfactory than the division, according to which each of the daughters will receive a share and Lear will be enabled to set his rest on the "kind nursery" of Cordelia.

Even if Lear had misgivings about making his daughters his masters, he would be considering himself rather than his kingdom. Their fitness to rule must to some extent be assumed, since they are going to rule anyway, or one of them is at least. Lear could hardly assume this while remaining distrustful of his daughters' power over him. Our hindsight is, of course, a great deal better than Lear's foresight, and we find fault with him for failing to see in advance what long familiarity with the play enables us to anticipate.

The precise nature of Lear's mistake, however, eludes the simple definition. It is a very complex mistake that is hidden under the curt decisiveness of the King as he alters his plan "upon the gad," disowns Cordelia, banishes Kent, circumscribes his power and makes himself dependent on Goneril and Regan. The impulsive king, the blind and foolish father — these leap too readily to mind. They are simple explanations at the moment, we might almost say obvious, but a huge and powerful drama lies before us to dispute what we are quick to say now. How blind is Lear? If we try to answer by citing the consequences of what he does, we shall rouse more difficulties than we settle. If we confine ourselves to the scene of which we are speaking, we will find the light a bit duller than we would like it to be yet sufficient to see what many overlook in their concentration upon what is to come.

We are considering the original plan of Lear and whether it is a political blunder. When he alters this plan, as a result of Cordelia's refusal to flatter him, are we right in thinking the second plan a political blunder, and if so, why? If Lear could reasonably suppose Goneril and Regan to be capable of wise and just rule in a three-fold division, why could he not assume the same thing in a two-fold division? I am speaking only of *political* considerations, nothing else. Much of the commentary on this point is so slipshod and superficial that I may appear to be laboring over fine distinctions in what many have blurred with hasty assumptions. The wrong which Lear does is not political in nature, though it does have wide repercussions in the world about him. Those who have reason to fear the consequences express doubts as to the love of the two older sisters for their father, and nothing about how they may wield the power they have just been granted. Kent says:

And your large speeches may your deeds approve,
That good effects may spring from words of love.

And a little later Cordelia says:

Use well our father.
To your professed bosoms I commit him.
But yet, alas, stood I within his grace,
I would prefer him to a better place.

The interrelation between love and political power is a highly significant one in the tragedy of *Lear*, but we can appreciate the connection only if we view each one by itself. The astuteness of authority on one side and the impulses of honest love on the other are two entirely separate entities, and it is an unpardonable error to confuse the two by implying that a violation of the second is a kind of ineptitude in the first. How blind is Lear? In his role as king he is no more blind than others around him. Neither Kent nor Cordelia has any more foresight — in the purely political sense — than Lear has. Kent's ringing exhortation "See better, Lear" concerns the filial love of Cordelia and has nothing whatever to do with political arrangements.[5]

The evidence is all against the notion, so often insisted upon, that the division of the kingdom is a piece of folly by a senile or self-centered monarch. Even the two-fold division is not politically unwise if we consider all the things Lear must reasonably have assumed in his plan to divide in three. If we are to infer from his actions now the kind of ruler he has been in the past, we can find no cause against him so far. Furthermore, we judge him fairly if we look to his original intention, the details of which must have taken a considerable while and necessitated pains-taking work with mapmakers, surveyors, advisers and so on. Whatever dangers we can foresee would in some sense have been mitigated by that arrangement. Though Lear continues to live with merely the title and all the addition to a king, and dwell with Cordelia in the most opulent third of the realm, he would in some way be a steadying influence. The royal power would not disappear altogether in the merely nominal status Lear intends to provide for himself, and the fitness of the daughters to rule would be tested under supervision, as it were, the kingly sway living on independently of anyone's power to strip it. Lear entertains no doubts as to his elder daughter's fidelity to him, but even the most unlikely eventualities would have their safeguard. All conditions for the transfer of power seem to have been perfectly worked out to insure continuance of rule as just and as safe as human ingenuity can devise.

We cannot, of course, establish the greatness of Lear as a royal sovereign on the strength of his plan to divide the kingdom. But we do refute the notion that he is foolish. If, then, it be asked precisely what there is about him in this opening scene that would impress us as truly imposing, my answer is that the staging and the acting of Lear himself must accord with what is made quite plain in the acts following. I recall a former professor of mine saying that the difficulty many people have in understanding why everyone believes Iago is that they imagine him as a typical kind of stage villain, smirking, shifty-eyed, gloating in every feature at the lies he is telling. Obviously, Iago does not act this way at all. If he did, we would wonder at the gullibility, not only of Othello, but of Desdemona, Cassio and Emilia as well. Yet it is impossible to single out specific lines or details to demonstrate that "honest Iago" has a straightforward manner which fools everyone into believing him. It is simply that one type of mannerism fits the substance of the play; the other does not, though the text does not make this clear till some time after Iago's initial appearance on stage.

The reverence for Lear is dramatised later, in fact severely tested under danger and duress, and yet it remains constant. What occasions this reverence? If there is only one scene in which Lear appears in all his glory and power, that scene should radiate something, without which the turmoil and passion of later scenes were pointless.

When he first steps before us, there is nothing of the senile or foolish old man that so many commentators have inferred from the folly of which he will shortly be guilty. His language is commanding and dignified. Four score years and upward he is, but a man who spends his days hunting, who will not surprise us that he is able to withstand the fury of the nightly storm, who exits running from attendants who have been sent after him, who kills the one that is hanging his daughter. His constitution is rugged. Physically, he is in excellent shape for a man of his years. There is no indication of incipient dotage, of the Polonius or any other variety. Even his reaction to what he regards as an insult, as well as the madness into which he falls, is essentially that of a powerful, if somewhat headstrong, mind rather than a weak or debilitated one. Every line of his bearing justifies what the disguised Kent says later:

. . . you have that in your countenance which
I would fain call master.

The more we visualize this monarch about to bestow a
kingdom the more we are impressed with the power he
holds and the grave confidence of his manner. This is the
man who will go insane and run bareheaded through the
lightning and thunder! The mere thought is enough to set
our blood tingling. The reality, when it occurs, will do
more than that. How the drama is enfeebled by imagining
this central figure as a pathetic old man or as a selfish
autocrat accustomed to have his own way and swim always
in flattery! What groundless theories have been fashioned
to sustain this meager concept, greatly inferior to the real
one and incompatible with the story that is his? Is it any
wonder that the play has been criticized as loosely knit,
improbable and poorly motivated?

The Lear that I see here is the one that Alfred Harbage
has well summed up:

Let us see him as he is, no preconceptions or
critical rumors spoiling the innocence of our
vision. Nothing about him suggests infirmity
or decay. . . . He issues commands with the
assurance of instinct and lifelong custom.
He holds a map in his hands like a Titan
holding a kingdom. . . . Thus he disposes of
a sector of the earth, this ring-giver, this
warrior-leader, this chosen one, his only
landlord God! Is it not passing fine . . . ?
Here is no soft-brained *Senex*, but the archetypal *King*.[6]

The supreme eminence of the king image is not something that Shakespeare chose to *teach* in King *Lear*. He
accepted it to begin with and had no reason to doubt that
his audience accepted it. The play does not set out to

prove a thesis; it assumes the thesis as true and proceeds accordingly.

The problem of accepting the king image lies not so much in substantiating its very natural bearing on the play — the most elementary knowledge of history will do it — but in post-royalty attitudes which make it difficult for us to share with the characters of the play (and with Shakespeare's audience) the veneration bestowed upon a king. The historical approach is helpful but not altogether satisfactory. We know that people of certain eras held the king in very high esteem. When a king is rejected, dispossessed, and driven out to run bareheaded in a storm, the effect upon the subjects who remain loyal is understandable. We regard them with a certain amount of sympathy, as we would look on natives weeping over the broken images of gods we do not ourselves believe in.

The king image will not of itself explain the high regard in which his subordinates hold him, but it will explain the low opinions many scholars have fashioned. In rejecting the king image, they reject Lear. As a kind of historical curiosity, annointed majesty may now be looked upon with detachment, amounting at times almost to disdain, whereas the man beneath the royal robes becomes an interesting study in hyman psychology. Many have busied themselves with the subject of Lear's madness, endeavoring to fix upon its earliest manifestations and the precise point at which he crosses the borderline from sanity to insanity. Interesting though the psychological states of Lear's mind may be, in a dramatic sense they are important only when related to the very thing that is so much neglected: that august and venerable king who is the tragic hero of the play.

Shakespearean drama abounds in unworthy kings as well as worthy kings, fit kings and unfit, successful ones and failures. In all cases the royal image counts for much but does not become a paramount consideration that transcends the failings of the man himself. Richard II, Cymbeline, Leontes have all become king without usurping the title, so that there is no question but that they are the rightful rulers. This fact does not blind the subjects to whatever faults may be found in the royal personage, however, any more than Lear's subjects are blind to *his* faults. As early as the opening scene we have intimations, inconclusive only to the extent that evidence is always sketchy at the beginning of a play, that Lear is esteemed as no other king is in Shakespeare.

This is the answer to those who say our first impression of Lear is a mean one and is drawn from the division of the kingdom (frequently misinterpreted) and the love test. They are wrong. The first impression — and it is an *impression* only — comes prior to both of these. The man we see is every inch a king, not some pitiful dotard whose mistake is in character. The very grandeur of this king makes his folly the more deplorable and its consequences the more disastrous. The effort to make Lear consistent goes against the very evident fact that there is a huge inconsistency here, one that we can explain and even come to understand, but not on the grounds that it is typical. [7]

We are about to embark on a very tragic history. What Lear signifies for some in the turmoil that follows and what he fails to signify for others will be pitted against each other in what seems like an uneven contest. The one side becomes solidly entrenched in power. The other is scattered, exiled, disguised for its own safety, yet loyal to the King, who is himself an outcast. The truth of life, as the play brings out so dramatically, consists in discovering what will work and what will not, what will bring forth evil and what will bring forth good, what will survive and what will perish. This truth exists independently of any rituals or ceremonials in which it may be expressed. Far from being no more than a heaving chaos which, for practical purposes, must be disguised, it emerges when all forms have been swept away and it secures the final victory in spite of the defeats it suffers in the process.

II

THE LOVE TEST

If the way in which Lear "tests" his daughters' affections is not actually the first impression we have of him, it is certainly one of the earliest and it comes very shortly after he makes his appearance on stage. He enters at line 34. At line 52 he asks the question:

Which of you shall we say doth love us most?

To a certain extent those critics may be pardoned who see the question and the way in which he accepts the answers as our first insight into the King's character. Indeed, it follows hard upon. What precisely is revealed, however, would bear considerable pondering, and if I treat it as the all-important first impression I do so for the sake of argument only and not because I have yielded the point I made in the preceding chapter.

Shakespearean characterization is vast and complex, as we should all be well aware by the time we come to read *King Lear*. We are not limited by what we see at any one time, significant though it may be, nor do we interpret so strictly as to allow no variation from what we call the, *significant act*. This kind of rigid simplicity is not the same thing at all as consistency. A certain mode of behavior, we will say, is in character, not because the individual never swerves from it, but because it arises from certain traits of which the action is one — but only one — manifestation. Thus, Angelo's attempted seduction of

17

Isabella in *Measure for Measure* is in character, not because Angelo has spent his entire life seducing religious novices, but because of a certain vulnerability which his pride would not permit him to see. Looking at it one way, we do detect a perplexing contradiction, but the more we reflect the more we see that human nature is revealed to an extent impossible in characters more simply conceived. Tartuffe is a hypocrite in every word and action; Angelo is a hypocrite only once. What greater depth of meaning there is in Shakespeare's portrayal than in Moliere's, with all due respect to the latter!

To impose Moliere's brand of uniformity upon Shakespeare is to conclude that Lear is accustomed to flattery and becomes highly irascible when he does not get it, that throughout his life he has mistaken flattery for love, and that his eventual rejection by the two evil daughters is a sort of condign punishment. While this interpretation is not without some element of truth, it ranges far beyond the evidence, to the point of contradicting it, in assuming that Lear has always acted in much the way we see him doing with Goneril and Regan and then with Kent and Cordelia.

Now when some exceptional mode of behavior occurs at the beginning of a play it is more likely to confuse than if it were to occur later. However, we must be aware of another consideration: the circumstances under which the action is performed. If they are in any sense unusual, we relate the action at least as much to them as to the character involved, particularly if there are positive indications that his action is unprecedented.

All this sounds more complicated than it actually is. It is a very normal thing to withhold judgment on characters and incidents when we are first becoming acquainted with the rudimentary beginnings of plot, and we proceed with the same caution even as we come to know more. Subconsciously we accept mysterious unknowns as very natural at the openings of any work of fiction, expecting that as the story unfolds we will be informed of what we need to know. Observe the lines with which the play begins:

> KENT. I thought the King had more affected
> the Duke of Albany than Cornwall.
> GLO. It did always seem so to us. But now,
> in the division of the kingdom, it appears
> not which of the Dukes he values most, for
> equalities are so weighed that curiosity
> in neither can make choice of either's
> moiety.

These lines are clear as far as they go, but we do not know who the Dukes of Albany and Cornwall are, and we are likely to think that the kingdom is to be divided in half rather than in thirds. The first scene of *The Tempest* is complete mystery, deliberately set forth to whet our curiosity, which in turn will be satisfied in Prospero's explanation at the beginning of the scene following. What applies to more elementary matters like plot introduction and identification of *dramatis personae* is true of the finer points of character development. The only thing that is clear at the moment is what we actually see and hear, and while it must in some way be consistent with what happens later, we look sharply at what takes place now and await further elaboration.

It is this consideration that seems to have escaped many who have discoursed so freely on what the love test is supposed to imply. The occasion is of paramount importance: after many long years of rule, Lear has reached the age at which he will retire and turn over the kingdom to his daughters. It is one of the last milestones in the life of the King, and we may wonder more at the absence of sorrow than at the display of tenderness. It is a dramatic moment and a susceptible one. What passes through his mind we can only guess, as he beholds the three daughters whom he loves so much, the youngest more than the other two, and is about to pass onto them what has been his for years beyond the life span of many present. Another man might weep at such a moment. Lear is royally impressive and dignified, but we cannot think that he is untouched by some emotion now that the ceremony is about to begin. He asks his famous question in a moment of parental fondness — fondness in the Elizabethan sense as well as our own — brought on by what he is about to do. Any father will recognize in Lear's request a perfectly normal desire, or smile at a very understandable weakness: the wish to be reassured of love even though there are no doubts that it exists. The very expression "love test" hardly applies. In the light of what comes to pass we may see deeper reasons for Lear's need to be reassured, but we must remember his stunned surprise when he eventually learns, as if for the first time, of Goneril's and Regan's lack of affection. Never does he give the slightest hint that secret forebodings have prompted him to give this "test." Consequently, we can assume that the only discernible reason for bidding his daughters speak their love is a very human emotion and relates to the all-important transfer about to take place.

It is of the greatest importance that we see this. The occasion, not the character of the King, inspires the question. Cordelia's asides do not suggest that her father has long been in the habit of demanding the flattery which she is unwilling to give. Supposing that he has been, we cannot avoid a few obvious questions. If Lear has always been accustomed to flattery, has Cordelia dutifully complied in the past? If so, why does she refuse now? If she has refused in the past, why does Lear love her most? — assuming, of course, that he has consistently taken flattery as evidence of affection.

The answer is that Lear has not been that kind of father, nor has Cordelia ever been faced with the disagreeable duty of refusing to humor him. She is faced with it now, for reasons that we shall see, but they have nothing to do with the King's past character as many have reconstructed it.

Rather than theorizing about an excessively domineering father so as to render his actions here part of a simple and well defined pattern, let us turn our attention to the occasion itself. The scene is one of regal pomp and magnificence. The stage is crowded. There is a flourish at the entry of Lear. Outside, the King of France and the Duke of Burgundy, rival suitors for the hand of Cordelia, await the answer Lear means to give them now. There will be another flourish when they enter in the company of those who attend upon them. Nothing in the scene suggests an intimate family gathering. Everything is gravely formal. The disposition of the kingdom has already been decided upon, as the opening lines of Kent and Gloucester have indicated, and this is to be the public ceremony at which the actual transfer will be made. It is in the midst of this stately splendor that Lear poses his question. When we behold the setting we do detect a strange anomaly and even have some incoherent misgivings. The sentimental feelings of a father intrude upon the solemnity of a royal court.

I am in substantial agreement with those who maintain that Lear did not plan this so-called love test and that it comes as a surprise to everyone. No one expresses any criticism, now or later — Cordelia and Kent speak out against the lavish answers of Goneril and Regan, not the question Lear asks — but this could be due to a general acceptance of the royal prerogative: kings are treated with a certain permissiveness. But since, as many have pointed out, the division of the kingdom has already been decided and no conditions have been set regarding a love test or any other kind of test, we can assume that the question occurs to Lear on the spur of the moment and, despite the way he asks it, with no bearing on who will get the most opulent third. The unconventionality of it suggests a paternal tenderness forcing itself into a rigidly formal setting, and if others on stage sense this they will think no worse of the King for it.

Yet even honest sentiment can be embarrassing when publicly displayed. Lear asks the question in kindness rather than with choking emotion, so that the embarrassment is of the mildest. The royalty of Lear graces such things, without making them disappear.

If we are thus afforded an insight into the heart of Lear at this moment, the august bearing of kingship softening perceptibly in the emotion of fatherhood, we will perhaps see in a new light the smooth-faced answers of the evil daughters. It is not simply that what they say is exaggerated beyond all truth, with the implication that Lear ought to recognize the fact, but that their perfectly controlled manner contrasts markedly with their father's vulnerable affection. Neither he nor they are prepared for this. But the mild impropriety of Lear in asking which of his daughters loves him most implies a certain honesty of feeling, just as their grand eloquence — more in keeping with the royal setting — has the ring of falsity. Goneril, the first to reply, has no chance to think about what she will say. But the ease with which she speaks suggests that she is not the least bit discomposed by any such emotion as seems to have prompted her father. To any sympathetic observer her answer, while it satisfies the King, is in quite another key from the question it is supposed to be answering.

Is it possible to answer such a question with honesty — with *emotional* honesty as well as moral? I believe that Cordelia senses the difficulty because she is naturally sympathetic and understands how, in spite of his majestic poise, her father has revealed his parental tenderness. She is not the one to laugh at sentimentality. But if she reads

22

the heart of her father and then the heart of her sister, she has reason to dread her turn to speak. Worse than laughing at sentimentality is the cool calculation that a lie will serve the purpose, let anyone attempt who will to point out its untruthfulness. If Cordelia alone were required to answer, without having to compete with her sisters, undoubtedly she could tell of her love in such a way that her very sincerity would alone be sufficient. But the lie has been told:

What shall Cordelia do? Love, and be silent.

Who would not resent the obvious advantage the elder daughters are taking of paternal tenderness? The game they are playing is too detestable to take part in, even to protect her father. Royal Lear, plunged into uncontrollable rage and running bareheaded through the storm is better to contemplate than a foolish old man awaiting the outcome of a battle of wits among his three daughters. This latter is not the father whom Cordelia has loved. Her intuition tells her that it is better to love him as she has always done, though it lose her his liking.

Those who consider Cordelia blunt and unfeeling do not see the difficulty under which she labors, nor even — as the text makes quite plain — that she would rather not answer at all. She certainly does not blurt out the word "Nothing." As the question is directed first to Goneril and then to Regan and finally to Cordelia, she knows it is now her turn to answer. Lear asks her:

... what can you say to draw
A third more opulent than your sisters?

She does not reply. Her father must prod her:

Speak.

He has not had to use this word with either Goneril or

Regan, who have answered him right away.[8] Cordelia's reluctance to say anything at all is an indication of the dilemma in which she is placed, and not of the blunt candor of which she is sometimes accused. It is also an indication that the situation is unusual and not typical. She undoubtedly has some foreboding that in wounding the father she will provoke the wrath of the king, as indeed turns out to be the case and which she would do anything to avoid, except become untruthful.

There are those who doubtless agree with Stoll's interpretation:

> Who could be more uncompromising than Cordelia or more provocative than Kent, though they know the nature of the King's other daughters into whose clutches they are thus throwing him? Characters so fine and devoted as they and the King, too, later show themselves to be could not at the outset have acted so in real life . . .[9]

This, of course, presumes the old error: a senile king, or at best a foolish and incompetent old man who must be protected by his daughter. If we read the King that way, we are more or less committed to reading Cordelia and Kent much the way that Stoll does. Yet in this very passage we are told of a contradiction — "Characters so fine and devoted as they . . . could not at the outset have acted so in real life . . ." In other words the characters are inconsistent, or at least are not real-life characters. Precisely. The loosely knit play again!

We might imagine Cordelia scolding her father as if he were a naughty child, and warning him that he had better mind her if he does not want to get in trouble. Not even those most convinced of Lear's senility would consider such a ridiculous idea, yet we do not avoid it merely by disguising it. Cordelia respects her father too much to assume the role of guardian, the more insulting since she would presumably keep him in ignorance — *for his own good!* A man who is definitely in the decline, who is barely able to take care of himself, whose judgment has lapsed into old age simplicity — in a word the kind of Lear whom Lamb rejected — would inspire affection more maternal than filial, as indeed the demented and overspent Lear inspires in Cordelia toward the end. In the reconciliation between father and daughter, that kind of affection is appropriate and has dramatic significance of its own. We miss something of the point of the play if we demand that Cordelia perform now what belongs elsewhere. The Lear we see before us is one who can be loved and revered but not pitied. It amazes me to read on the one hand of Cordelia's coldness, and then to read condemnation of the reconciliation scene for being sentimental, as if we ought to reverse Shakespeare and have Cordelia sentimental rather than honest in the opening scene, and then unmoved in a situation in which honest sentiment is both natural and good. The feelings of Cordelia are as truthful as the words she utters. Never does she stoop to cajolery. Loving her father as she does, she is perfectly sincere when she says that she "would prefer him to a better place" than the professed bosoms of her sisters, but the desirability of this end cannot justify any means however bad.

If Cordelia were "tactful," the play would collapse. In a practical world the practical reason will always obtrude itself. Obviously, any dramatist is aware that his characters must do and say things without which there would be no play. Actions, however, must be consistent with character and not merely a device for precipitating catastrophe. Where there is an evident inconsistency between what a character is and what the dramatist makes him do in order to develop the plot, we think ill of both plot and character. No play is successful when it is illogically motivated, regardless of how interesting or exciting the action that follows. When characters do things simply because the result will be dramatic conflict, the device becomes immediately transparent. Characters who are unconvincing cannot interest us, regardless of the seeds of discord they manage to sow. Even one glaring inconsistency cannot be overlooked, though the rest of the play be perfect.

If Cordelia were to speak her love, truthfully, it would sound very cold and flat after what her sisters have said. That she does eventually tell of her love, in response to her father's insistence, shows this. She can avoid the unfavorable contrast only by equaling or surpassing her sisters, and thus dismissing as inconsequential one of the supremely tender and sacred moments of Lear's entire life. Love would have no real importance where a lie might serve a practical end. This is the "tact" we would have her exercise.

To understand the deeper meaning of love is not to exonerate Lear. On the contrary, he is chargeable with folly which I do not mean to extenuate. I wish merely to dispute the allegations of senility, creeping madness, lifelong despotism, any or all of which we must presume if we insist that Cordelia might have behaved with better grace. What intuitions trouble her as it becomes her turn to speak we can guess with some likelihood. She, not her sisters, will have the care of their father. Which of her two suitors, the Duke of Burgundy or the King of France, will become her husband? Doubtless she is better acquainted with them than we are from the short while they are on stage, and can see in the practical-minded Burgundy a possible source of future difficulty should he in any way resent her father, as she seems to divine that her sisters will. Could she, in whatever conflict might arise, prove herself an enemy to all other joys and find her sole felicity in her dear Highness' love? What reproaches might Lear speak if she were to fall short then of what he apparently wants her to say now? Cordelia does not know the answers to these things. Womanlike, she probably does not even ask herself the questions, but realizes in her heart that the married state is yet a mystery to her and that the lord whose hand must take her plight has some claim to her love, her care and duty. If she has even the remotest misgivings she has reason to say, " . . .what I well intend I'll do't before I speak." To declare lavishly and then fail in what sounds like a holy vow does not bother Goneril in the least. Nor Regan. But Cordelia is made of different clay.

It is utterly beyond me how some have formed the most disparaging opinions of Cordelia as a result of her refusal to follow her sisters' lead. What is often characterized as her "blunt refusal to flatter" we may try to soften by supposing her to be unthinking or to have been provoked into blurting her famous "Nothing" in a moment of resentment. This kind of defense in reality admits the charge but pleads extenuating circumstances. It is the charge which is false, and extenuating circumstances so-called must really be improvised — like Lear's discreditable past — to explain what is contradictory. Almost two hundred lines elapse from the time she first answers her father to the time that she leaves the stage. She has ample time to reflect. The full and terrible consequences are made clear. Neither here nor anywhere else in the play does she appear to be thoughtless or capable of even the mildest kind of ire, but even if she were liable to either one, the moment passes and the outcome might certainly convince her that she had spoken words she did not really mean. Why does she not admit, if only to herself, that she ought to have expressed herself differently?

Pride, as we all know, can make a holy cause of the worst blunder or the most gratuitous insult. But pride alone will not suffice when there is injury to other people. Does Cordelia suffer qualms of conscience, yet say nothing because her pride is more important to her than her

father's happiness is? If we account thus for her persist-
ence, we must accuse her of something worse than pride.
Branson does not really stop to think when he says she is
cold in this scene, but learns more about love during her
period of exile.[10] We know nothing of what takes place
while she is living in France, and even Branson tells us that
she is already beginning to change toward the end of the
scene, thereby accounting for her tears as she takes her
leave while preferring her father to a better place than the
"professed bosoms" of her older sisters. Her tears, in point
of fact, are not tears of remorse, nor could she conceivably
be learning *more* about love only now or during her stay in
France to come. She does not regret what she has said but
the way in which it has been received and acted upon.

Those who defend Cordelia tell us that she is disgusted
with her father's obvious desire for flattery and refuses to
satisfy it. However, she speaks not a word that would
suggest this, and the supposed bluntness with which she
speaks is not motivated by any disagreeable sentiments
toward her father. When he speaks scornfully of her to
Burgundy and France, she defends herself:

> I yet beseech your Majesty —
> If for I want that glib and oily art,
> To speak and purpose not, since what I well intend
> I'll do't before I speak — that you make known
> It is no vicious blot, murder, or foulness,
> No unchaste action or dishonored step,
> That hath deprived me of your grace and favor,
> But even for want of that for which I am richer,
> A still-soliciting eye, and such a tongue
> As I am glad I have not, though not to have it
> Hath lost me in your liking.

This is said in explanation and not attack, whatever words
of scorn she uses being applied to her sisters and not to her

father. Even the King of France finds her position a reasonable one:

> Is it but this? A tardiness in nature
> Which often leaves the history unspoke
> That it intends to do?

France's opinion of her is not compromised in the least by what Lear regards as sufficient cause to disown her:

> She is herself a dowry.

Certainly he has no fears as to her coldness or her failure to understand the nature of love. He to whom love is "not love when it is mingled with regards that stand aloof from the entire point" might be expected to have some worthy ideas on the subject.

Cordelia has not refused to say how much she loves her father. She has simply refused to lie about it. The "bond" to which she refers and which she will neither exceed nor neglect is not a mere legal requirement; it is, like other bonds that are violated during the course of the play, a sacred one which she honors deeply. Married or single, a daughter loves her father most ideally when she loves according to their proper relationship, nor more nor less.

Let it be understood that, although Cordelia speaks of the man she will marry carrying *half her love with him,* she is using a figure of speech rather than an applicable mathematical formula. Love, as she would be the first to insist, is not a measurable quantity that must be cut in half when it is given to two people instead of one. Possibly there is a bit of irony in her terms of measurement, her father insisting on knowing "how much" and her sisters replying with Miltonic comparisons. A return to proportions somewhat more modest, though it may entail a philosophical contradiction, has a common-sense edge cutting through the lofty verbiage of Goneril and Regan.

Cordelia is herself living proof that her affection for Lear is not in any sense halved in order to make place for the man she accepts in marriage. But when Goneril claims that her love is "Beyond what can be valued, rich or rare," and when Regan insists that even this "comes too short," well may Cordelia wonder, "Why have my sisters husbands . . .?" The nature of each affection is unique and, within its own limits, may be immeasurable. Whereas, two romantic attachments (as Goneril, Regan and Edmund demonstrate by their actions), two fatherly loves — if we can imagine such a predicament — are a violation of nature. One interferes with the other, and only in such cases can we think of love being divided.

The soul of Cordelia is not inclined to such analysis. The arithmetical terms she uses may be intentional irony, or may be a kind of philosophical falsity born of inexperience. She has not yet loved, maritally, and is in the delicate position of not knowing which of the two suitors at court, if indeed either of them, will be her husband, but her heart is right and we detect truth rather than error in her analogy. Cordelia is intuitive, but she is innocent. Of one thing she is certain: she loves her father as is "right fit." A partial carrying out of her duty to him will be in a marriage that he will desire and bless. What she will do then must proceed from a heart that is sincere in all things, and the best evidence she can give now is to stand aloof from those hyperboles that would confuse, encroach upon and annihilate all other forms of love. The heart is a better judge than the head.

"That little seeming substance," as Lear scathingly refers to her, is true in a way that would make him marvel if only he had eyes to penetrate her soul. A maiden so young and slight amid the sparkle of royalty, the dignity of patriarchal age, the representatives of foreign political power, to harbor within herself the conflict she will not divulge but which in time will reveal its nature in explosive convulsions and shake the whole world of man! We find it difficult to believe, just as many criticize the play for being inadequately motivated. Too much comes from too little. The intense drama of the middle section is traced to a domestic spat in the first scene, a mere tempest in a teapot.[11] Such nearsighted criticism, though it sees clearly enough a certain disparity of events, is blurred on the purposed design of the author in rendering them disparate, or presumably so.

The love test is not a deliberate allegory or a symbolic representation, the kind of extravaganza that could be staged in tableau. Not Lear, not Regan or Goneril, not even Cordelia or Kent is aware of the importance of the King's question or of the answers he receives. It all begins in an almost casual way, proceeding from nothing more than a father's desire to hear how much his children love him. The apparent disproportion between this and the mighty storm scenes, however, is a little too obvious to be an oversight by Shakespeare or the result of his creative powers running away with him. The atmosphere in which love is tested should be a clue to something more significant than a trivial episode in the life of an old man and his three daughters. Lear symbolizes authority: authority fully recognized and rightly venerated. As king and as father — those two eminent symbols by which all authority, divine as well as human, has long been depicted — and as a man whose great age makes him impressive rather than ridiculous, Lear is more than just a dramatic character with specific traits. Royalty could find no better image than Lear crowned and robed in this one striking scene. Authority he certainly is, from head to toe.

Now, Authority wonders how much it is loved. The question is neither unnatural nor unusual. After posing this question three times, to those over whom it rules in both capacities, king and father, it receives three answers: two in the voice of flattery and deceit, one in the voice of honesty and true love. Which will Authority prefer?

This harsh depersonalization of the action appears repellent at first, but the regal setting and the strange anomaly of the question suggests a relationship too long forgotten. The figures of this high drama are emblematic, but they come before us as human beings and never cease to be so. We go astray when we say they are emblematic *ratherthan* human, as if they could not be both, or as if their humanity makes it impossible to equate the vastness of love, hatred, truth, falsehood with the episodes that first bring them to light. The result is that we are forced to choose between two concepts when it is actually the combination that gives the play its titanic power and its vivid actuality.

In that grand patriarch Lear and in the youthful and innocent Cordelia we see the symbols of authority and love respectively. No two could be less alike. If we think in terms of the Elizabethan concept that authority as well as order depends ultimately on love, we find it difficult to apply here and see the impressive and powerful Lear as in some way depending upon that little seeming substance he views with such scorn. The day will come — but let us not anticipate. Authority may act its will with apparent impunity, become incensed at the truthfulness of love, dispossess love and turn its portion over to the forces of deceit. We hardly recognize the power of love in the helpless Cordelia, so easily victimized by her outraged father, nor does any force in the universe strike back at him for what he has done. The heavens do not fall. Authority is not diminished one bit except for what it voluntarily surrenders, but even the hastily revised plan of turning over the kingdom is subject to conditions that signify continuity of the old order rather than preparation for a new. How this may work out in practice remains to be seen, but the person of Lear continues to radiate a kind of inviolability. Our misgivings stem from the fact that the authority he now exercises is not unlike the health of a man who drinks a slowly working poison and continues to live and move about with ease.

Practical considerations are relevant, but even these call attention to the emblematic nature of what has taken place. Lear came to give away his kingdom and he intended to give it in love. When he divides Cordelia's share between Goneril and Regan, however, he does not give in love; he gives in rage. The reapportionment is punishment for Cordelia, not an additional reward for the other two. The meaning of this action on the part of Lear is seen vaguely at best if we become lost in the question as to whether a king may under any circumstances give up his power, yet retain the deference that has always been his due. The circumstances here are specific; they concern the basis on which the kingdom is to be allotted.

It is a truism that the meanings we must seek run much deeper than those which are prepared and given us without any effort on our part to find them. This is generally true of the plays of Shakespeare, though perhaps to none does it apply as it does to *King Lear*. A wealth of major characters, all drawn by the author at the height of his creative powers, engulfs us in clashing personalities — almost to the point of confusion. From what they do come meanings that are cosmic in significance! How do we relate these two?

The answer lies partly in the fact that the full import of this first scene is not understood by those involved in it. Neither Lear nor Cordelia analyzes love in its true relationship to power. He is guided at first by a very human feeling, and she reacts from a heartfelt instinct. The whole affair begins and ends on a mild note, the explosive climax in the middle is not anticipated, and after it has taken place there is no immediate result. Both Kent and Cordelia express doubts — but doubts only — as to the outcome. For the rest, the scene appears to be nothing more than a family matter, a terrible one to be sure that might have been avoided as most family quarrels can be: with a little tact. So it would seem. Truly they know not what they do. High principles or low guide the chief actors, but their view of eventualities is dim at best.

Wherein, then, lies the guilt of Lear? What is the extent of this guilt? Little can be said on this subject other than that he commits a great wrong which can be explained only in terms of psychological reasons, as many have already explained it: the pride of a powerful monarch has been wounded, publicly. He has listened to the sweet voice of flattery and prefers it to the voice of truth. The sin needs no interpretation. It is most meaningful when we regard it so, interpretation usually taking the form of unwarranted theories as to Lear's past or Cordelia's. A blunt sin, an unprecedented folly in a good and venerable king! This is what stuns us. The very gravity of the deed lies in the greatness rather than the littleness of the one who commits it, for guilt, like mercy, is mightiest in the mightiest.

It is with this thought, so briefly stated yet so incomprehensible, that we watch Lear leave the stage, and turn to look upon the weeping Cordelia bidding farewell to her sisters. Her words are the first expression of a love that remains constant in the face of the wrong Lear has committed, and spoken by the one who suffers most. When one continues to love in spite of the cruel treatment she receives from another, the one on whom she bestows her love is blest by it. So human is the story, that we overlook its symbolic meaning: Authority has banished Love, but Love has not banished Authority.

III

EDMUND

Edmund's famous soliloquy to Nature is a rejection of all those things by which the authority of Lear has existed and by which the person of Lear continues to be esteemed. The forms, the distinctions, the hierarchical ranks of civilized life are not, in Edmund's view, justified by anything in nature. If his dimensions are as well compact, his mind as generous and his shape as true as "honest madam's issue," why should he be considered in any wise inferior?

> Why brand they us
> With base? With baseness? Bastardy? Base, base?
> Who in the lusty stealth of nature take
> More composition and fierce quality
> Than doth, within a dull, stale, tired bed,
> Go to the creating a whole tribe of fops . . .

Edmund's line of reasoning is apparent at a glance. What gives its literal meaning even greater significance, however, is the precise moment at which it is given: directly upon the conclusion of the scene in which the King turns over the rule to Goneril and Regan. The apportionment is made and the scene is quietly concluded. Then the opportunist appears. The time is ripe.

Nahum Tate's version of the play begins with this soliloquy, somewhat altered but substantially the same, and the division of the kingdom takes place afterward. In thus rearranging the sequence of events Tate excludes any connection, it seems to me, between what Lear has done and what Edmund plans to do. Although the plan to divide the kingdom is known in advance by everyone (as it is in Shakespeare), and disapproved by both Gloucester and Kent, the test of love and the dispossessing of Cordelia do not take place till after Edmund has begun intimating to his father that Edgar is engaged in a wicked "plot." If we are to presume any connection at all between Lear's actions and Edmund's, in the Tate version it would have to be between the original plan of division and Edmund's sensing it as his opportunity. The love test could have nothing to do with either one. In Shakespeare, on the other hand, Lear's intention to retire from active rule and turn it over to his three daughters is not criticized by anyone, nor does it seem likely to have inspired ambitious thoughts in Gloucester's illegitimate son. What stirs Edmund is the division as it is actually made.

This is not to say that only now is Edmund beginning to think of rising beyond his station. We may wonder just how long these thoughts have been in his mind, as we may wonder how long Macbeth has dreamed of becoming King of Scotland. In each play something happens to convert daydreams into practical designs and from designs into action. With Edmund there is every indication that he has long thought upon what he says here and has been awaiting only the chance to act upon it. His speech is casual and self-assured, not the talk of a man struck for the first time with a very unconventional idea. His convictions on the subject of his own bastardy and the "plague of custom" are certainly borne of a life tainted by illegitimate birth and barred from those areas into which his aspiring thoughts have ventured. There is no such moral struggle as plagues Macbeth, by which we may see the difference between two men possessed of ambition, but one "without the illness should attend it." Edmund reacts immediately and calmly to what precipitates Macbeth into an unbearable turmoil of conscience. In such a readiness to act we may presume a mind long prepared and thoroughly conditioned. Our only question is, Why does he wait till *this* particular moment? His action is swift. He has already forged the letter that will ruin his brother and holds it now in his hand.

Perhaps the ripeness of the occasion is more effectively brought out by juxtaposition than by specific mention. Look here upon this picture, and on this. Reflect well upon what happened in the previous scene, and then consider what follows. While Edmund does not mention Lear, or anything for that matter that would give him his chance at long last, it is nonetheless clear—as subsequent events show—that his ambition goes much higher than becoming Earl of Gloucester. Nor is his philosophy of opportunism limited to the political climate only. It is a philosophy long pondered and expressed now in the form of a vow to reality as he conceives it—free from the curiosity of nations and all the artificial distinctions that man has contrived:

> Thou, Nature, art my goddess, to thy law
> My services are bound.

Coming directly after what we may call, for want of a better term, the allegory of violated love, Edmund's view of the world is related in more ways than opportunity. His soliloquy elaborates a far-reaching and all-inclusive concept of life itself and is comparable in magnitude to the view of life which it denounces. If we had no glimmerings before of what Lear means to the world of civilized man, we begin to see it in the entire catalogue of what Edmund rejects. If we were inclined to underestimate the distinction between true love and feigned, or inclined to imagine that a little tact would have patched up the difference, this blunt revelation will make us reconsider, and will drive the point home again and again as Edmund feigns devotion—to his father, to Edgar, to Cornwall, to Goneril, to Regan—for the same purpose these last two feigned it: to acquire all for one's own self. Edmund's stature grows as he talks, the implications of his belief—or rather *dis*-belief-extending to cosmic dimensions.

It is intentional, I believe, that Shakespeare presents no philosophical defense of the contrary view anywhere in the play. Edmund is perhaps the only "thinker." Those in the first scene who knew not what they did were simply acting according to a very common phenomenon of life, by which the virtuous foundations of society are but dimly remembered over the long existence of a well-regulated kingdom. Good and evil become relative terms. Honesty becomes a tactfulness to be exercised as the exigencies of the moment demand. Only the love of virtue, a rarity in sophisticated life, can prevent complete moral indifference and wage a continual struggle with moral forgetfulness.

I am not speaking of a corrupt society in which evil is rampant, but of a highly civilized society that still acknowledges right and wrong. It may laugh at adultery, as Gloucester does, without making it a general practice. Such a society is difficult to define with any accuracy. To point out what is wrong with it is to appear to be condemning it outright; to speak of its wrongs as understandable is to appear to be condoning it. When we say that a character like Edmund thrives on the kind of world in which he was born and raised, we do not mean—at least we *should* not mean—that he is a symbol of the evil which has nourished him. He is too unlike the other characters to be the quintessence of any wicked ways they may have and even those he most resembles—Goneril and Regan—he far surpasses in calculated malice and the artistry with which he perpetrates it.

The *indifference* of society, the *unconcern* – these terms are too strong. *Forgetfulness* is inexact. No one of them suggests the inactivity of what was once active, or the inattention where there was once a scrupulous perception. But Edmund's trenchant metaphysics comes as an eye-opener. It is incisive. It is clear. To many it goes so far as to be convincing. As Lear is old and represents a time-honored system, so Edmund is young and flourishes a new idea, not new as of the moment but new in the more slowly paced chronology of changing thought. Those who see in Lear's retirement the passing of an age will see in Edmund the dawn of a new one. His youthful energy and freshness are capable of blinding us to the nature of his beliefs and direct our attention to those that coincide with our own, such as his rejection of astrology. Next to Edmund, Lear looks outmoded.[12] Any attempt to evaluate the past, except on Edmund's terms, seems woefully unappealing. Such may be the mood into which we fall at the moment, regardless of what the past has meant and what the future is likely to mean. Time will do more than tell.

Those who admit Edmund Chorus to this history are so impressed with stature and philosophical disquisition, even some who disapprove, that their vision is blurred and they see nothing but the towering figure before them. He overwhelms them. The order presided over by royal Lear is indeed taken for granted and its true significance somewhat eclipsed in the absence of regal apologetics. It is true that, through passive acceptance, ceremonies and rituals have become, if not altogether meaningless, certainly a great deal less meaningful. This is one of the discoveries Lear makes when he divests himself of power and lives on as a king in ritual only.

It is idle either to dismiss the chaotic world into which Lear is thrust as a fantastic place in which improperly motivated people perform bizarre actions or to accept it as a portrait of inescapable reality. Shakespeare does not show us what always happens any more than he shows us what never happens; he shows us what *can* happen. As we witness the tragic story unfolding, we wonder what might have been if certain characters had acted differently or thought differently. Unless they are following out the foreordinations of fate or are behaving with complete irrationality, they act by some choice not entirely devoid of reason. This choice may be influenced by what is sometimes called a "ruling passion,"[13] without being compelled by it—which would simply be fate by another name. The fact of choice implies a great deal more inner reflection than would the concept of a passion that rules absolutely. Even when the act is performed suddenly and without allowing for time to think, such as Goneril's flattery for instance, it is not therefore the result of passion in any sense of the word, but rather of character itself as developed by a life of attitudes and preferences, at least as much as and perhaps more than the humors in the body. As the comedies of Ben Jonson show, humors can be feigned, which would be impossible if substances in the body were the sole determiner of character. What is true physically is also true emotionally and intellectually.

Thus do we regard Edmund as he first reveals himself to us. He is deliberative. He is a conscious plotter. He is a careful strategist, one who directs instead of being directed. His is not a reflex action to the opportunity that presents itself. Rather he is a natural seeker of opportunities and recognizes in them what most men fail to see.

To probe the mind of Edmund, both prior to the present time and as it has undoubtedly been influenced by the most recent developments, is enlightening. This close scrutiny of character is sometimes condemned as inconsistent with the live performance of a play, during which we have little time to consider Edmund's past. However, I believe that, since the attitudes of Shakespeare's day were very much alive in conversation and pamphlet, such a character would have been more quickly recognized than he is by today's theatre-goer.[14] Nevertheless, human psychology is substantially the same in all times, though what the cynical-minded may reject varies from age to age. While Edmund pledges his loyalty to *Natura,* which a modern nihilist would not do, the facts of his life and the two soliloquies he speaks—separated by some 105 lines on account of Gloucester's appearance—afford us ample opportunity to reflect upon why this man thinks as he does and to what extent the matter of the opening scene determines how high a pitch his resolution soars.

Though Edmund "came something saucily into the world before he was sent for," his childhood and youth must have been as happy as that of his brother Edgar, who, Gloucester says, "yet is no dearer in my account." Nowhere does Edmund say anything that would lead us to believe that he has been in any way neglected. Unquestionably his tainted birth has always rankled, much more, in fact, than his flippant references to it would indicate. When he gives his soliloquy he has already embarked on his quest to grow and prosper and has consigned to oblivion everything that would stand in his way. While his tone is self-assured, however, he protests overmuch, not unlike one who has chafed in the past over what seemed as unreasonable then as it does now:

—fine word, "legitimate"!

Such thoughts are not unusual with men who begrudge others what they themselves are denied and who compensate by sneering at those distinctions that render some men less and others greater. The human animal is often victim to such resentment. It may make one man morose and convert another to burning ambition. Whether the ambitious man will react to opportunity will depend to a large extent on what society itself believes. The question implicit in Edmund's soliloquy is "Why not?" If those about him were as evil as he is, he would not bother to ask the question. If they were potently virtuous, the answer would be obvious. But virtue which is habit, though it deserves our commendation, can make no answer—be it astrology or anything else—that Edmund would not dismiss as "the excellent foppery of the world."

The success that attends his strategy is likely to divert us to other conclusions, particularly in view of Edmund's own words:

> A credulous father, and a brother noble,
> Whose nature is so far from doing harms
> That he suspects none, on whose foolish
> honesty
> My practices ride easy.

Those who speak of the credulity of Gloucester, in believing so readily a plot by a son whom he has always loved, overlook the state of mind he is in as he enters:

> Kent banished thus! And France in choler
> parted!
> And the King gone tonight! Subscribed his
> power!
> Confined to exhibition! All this done
> Upon the gad!

Lear's precipitate action may be expected to have consequences, it is too early to say exactly what, but Gloucester's nervous apprehension is likely to accept rather than reject any report of further evil. Later he speaks of the changing times, an indication that the benefits which sacred bonds confer upon society are now beginning to disappear:

> Love cools, friendship falls off, brothers
> divide. In cities, mutinies; in countries,
> discord; in palaces, treason; and the bond
> cracked 'twixt son and father.

While this second passage is spoken as a result of Edgar's supposed treason, the facts were certainly in Gloucester's mind prior to learning of the forged letter. Certainly without blame, Gloucester was yet victim of a psychological condition which, once yielded to, is not recognized afterward for the temporary thing it was. The times may have gone bad on something more than a temporary basis, but Gloucester's mood is one that would pass if he were given nothing more to worry about. As it is, he is all but certain from this moment forward. Though he does yield somewhat to Edmund's hypocritical pleas that he withhold his judgment, he twice refers to Edgar as "villain," and we seriously wonder how necessary is the additional proof which Edmund offers in a later scene. Gloucester is at fault, but his action is not incomprehensible, nor can we agree with Tolstoy that the "relations between Gloucester and his two sons, and the feelings of these characters, are as unnatural as Lear's relation to his daughters, or even more so . . ."[15]

Another matter which has received too much attention and which also diverts us from the central purpose of this scene is the astrology of Gloucester. Now, as regards his "superstition," upon which many have built such a seemingly convincing case, the reasons he gives for believing "We have seen the best of our time" is not really the late eclipses. Read the speech:

> These late eclipses in the sun and moon portend no good to
> us. Though the wisdom of nature can reason it thus and
> thus, yet nature finds itself scourged by the sequent
> effects. Love cools . . . This villain of mine comes under
> the prediction . . .

He believes the times to be bad because of the facts he cites rather than because the late eclipses, which he mentions only briefly, have frightened him into believing that they are.

Edmund is far more detailed in rejecting astrology than his father is in accepting it. The great psychological fact of rationalism attacking a passive kind of faith is set forth in these few speeches. Rationality is all on the side of the negativist; gullibility, so-called, is all on the other side. If we see no more than this, we are impressed with the philosophical astuteness of Edmund and the somewhat senile attachment of his father to an untenable faith in astrological phenomena. The "sequent events," however, while they may be difficult to cite as justification for Gloucester's concern over the late eclipses, are actually more in line with his supposed credulity than with Edmund's cynical incredulity. Gloucester does actually admit that "the wisdom of nature can reason it thus and thus," suggesting that there are two sides to the question. Edmund is self-assured and positive. He savors the full pleasure of rejection.

Since his repudiation of astrology is spoken after his decision has been made and his machinations have already begun to work as well as he could wish, it has no such purpose as deliberating the issues or strengthening his own convictions. All of Edmund's "philosophy," if we may call it that, is given in this scene. From now on everything he says, including his private meditations, have a practical object in view. Yet he is capable of abstract thought, and, since he indulges it only here, we may infer the existence of a supreme moment in his life. Though other villains in Shakespeare may approach Edmund in the practicality of their designs, none surpasses him. None takes swifter advantage of unexpected turns of events than he does, or with fewer words. Nor has any villain devoted his life to evil with less apparent motivation than he. Those who, like Macbeth and Claudius, kill in order to further their ambitions are not calculating criminals in the sense that Iago and Richard 111 are. Iago resents being passed over when Othello names Cassio his lieutenant, and in addition believes, or pretends to believe, an affair has taken place between Othello and Emilia. Richard 111 is convinced that, now that the wars are over, his physical deformity bars him from all "delight to pass away the time." Only in evil can he seek fulfillment:

> To entertain these fair well-spoken days,
> I am determined to prove a villain
> And hate the idle pleasures of these days.

In each case a dialectical discourse that evil prospers more than good is an outlet for anger upon all the world. Each man hates, not in towering rage, but in that far more dangerous and insidious way of controlling the passions and allowing reason to direct hatred to its most effective fulfillment.

Edmund does not hate anyone. Even Don John, since he knows what it is to be illegitimate, directs his animosity wholly against Claudio, that young upstart who "hath all the glory of my overthrow." The absence of this specific kind of incentive in Edmund makes him stand out. When we seek the reason for his actions we must seek something infinitely greater than personal injury or brooding over what he is or envy of another. No adversary or group of adversaries drives him to bitter thoughts of retaliation. He has no enemies. His mention of his brother is brief and to the point—"I must have your land"—and later his comment is simply that Edgar is one "on whose foolish honesty my practices ride easy." What villain could hate such a convenient brother? After he rids himself of Edgar, Edmund thinks no more about him.

Edmund feigns devotion to his father in a most effective way. Note the wording of the letter he has forged:

> I begin to find an idle and fond bondage in the oppression of aged tyranny, who sways not as it hath power, but as it is suffered.

Nothing could have come so directly from the heart of Edmund as this blunt statement about aged tyranny. A concocted lie is apt to sound like a lie. What one truly believes has the impact of solid substance. All Edmund has to do is transfer the guilt from himself to his brother, just as he does a few lines later when he says:

> . . . I have heard him oft maintain it to be fit that, sons at perfect age and fathers declining, the father should be as ward to the son, and the son manage his revenue.

This is probably what Edmund himself has long thought. He knows, of course, that it will provoke his father, and a father who is provoked is next door to believing the thing he resents. Resenting it, he is already more kindly disposed toward the son who disavows the other son's perfidy.

Edmund works through flattery, less obvious and infinitely more subtle than that practiced on Lear. He imputes an evil design to his brother. Though the brother allegedly came to him and broached his intent, Edmund professed an abiding loyalty to his father and a deep reverence for the bond between father and son:

... I told him the revenging gods
'Gainst parricides did all their thunders bend,
Spoke with how manifold and strong a bond
The child was bound to the father.

This of course is flattery a little more obvious. Edmund
has small respect for any such beliefs as that you cannot
gain honor for yourself by dishonoring others. He knows
that you can. To remain loyal despite another's disloyalty,
to be unmoved by offers of personal profit, is to prove
oneself under the hottest kind of temptation and to inspire
a new respect from all. But the devil must be in the affair
before it will work. Even the wound he inflicts upon his
arm dramatizes the indispensable relationship of villainy
and fidelity. The faithfulness we would exhibit to the
world becomes virtuous only when under attack:

Some blood drawn on me would beget opinion
Of my more fierce endeavor.

Thus do we watch Edmund rise. The moment he can
betray his father he does so. He accepts the love of Goneril
and then of Regan without emotional involvement. It is
not simply that moral distinctions mean nothing to him.
His personal feelings remain untouched. Even his soliloquy
on the question as to which of the sisters he will take, after
having sworn love to both, is a cold and practical
deliberation of policy. He feels no human antagonisms, no
lustful desires, none of the more understandable sins that
plague other men. His sinfulness does not appear to be an
aberration or a misuse of something good, as love turned
to lust, or moral condemnation turned to vindictiveness.

Edmund is indeed in advance of his time, not in the
sense that he anticipates some later phase of human
progress, but that his type does not usually appear until a
more advanced stage of decay has set in. The negative

analysis whereby he justifies his schemes is the kind of thinking that is usually caused by widespread corruption. This lends an appearance of righteousness to the apostate's ideas, which often deceives him as well as those around him. No such corruption exists in the play. Edmund's negativism is devoid of any pretense that he is turning his back upon a sinful world and seeking blessed freedom from the rules and prohibitions to which men pay lip service only. The power and meaning of his world view are what engage us, not any spurious justification of it. We understand something of the reasons for his decision, just as we understand the psychology of other forms of evil, but our attention is directed more toward the enormity of what he will do rather than any excuse he may have for doing it. The sins of society are less important, actually, than the good that still exists and which he plans to violate.

The rise of Edmund and the fall of Lear are perfectly counterpoised. As one is first treated with disrespect, then has his train diminished, next is made an outcast and finally is the subject of a plot against his life, the other becomes more esteemed, more trusted, is promised greater honors and is eventually on the brink of becoming the most powerful man in England. What Edmund stands for is very clearly stated and becomes more and more ominous as he gains power. What Lear stands for is never actually stated, but begins to loom larger and larger as he loses power. Though the two men rarely mention each other and their actions are not directly related, each casts a revealing light upon the other, so much so that Edmund's role truly enhances the royalty he would supplant.

Edmund speaks far more eloquently in his actions than he does in soliloquy, and as his star rises we cannot help thinking what he would have done had he attained his highest ambitions. Had he and Goneril murdered Albany, as they planned to do, and gotten rid of the widow Regan or held her in subjection, Edmund would have ruled Britain alone, he who plotted against his brother, ruined his father and gave the execution order for Lear and Cordelia. Whatever deterrent to his power might be looked for in Goneril, small as we can imagine it, would prove unavailing when we consider the cynical way he pretended to love her. Not the least of our questions would concern what possible satisfaction or sense of fulfillment Edmund is capable of. Unable to enjoy what he has attained on a lower scale, would he find contentment on the scale toward which his aspirations lead him? An unhappy or distrustful ruler, cynical of human fellowship, is likely to be a monster to his subjects. The energy that brought him to the throne can easily seek an outlet in the most malicious exploitation, if only to relieve the boredom of having no more worlds to conquer. For such a man there is no turning back. Murder confines him to the path he has taken. Having killed without qualms, he has his mind so set upon the thing he wants that he is shut out from all else. Remorse he cannot feel, only frustration. Unlike Claudius, who wishes to repent his crime but cannot bring himself to yield the crown and queen for which he did the murder, Edmund is of such a rigid cast of mind that he could undoubtedly watch undisturbed a reenactment of all his villainy, and then plan quietly to dispatch those who had found him out.

Edmund's thoughts and actions attest conclusively that he has committed himself to this kind of life. That such a fate lies in store for him is less evident than it would be if he had attained the goal, for the simple reason that the psychology of the plotter is not the same once he has succeeded and has everything for which he schemed, lied and murdered. Acquisition is pleasanter than possession, particularly in one whose own hard dealings teaches him to suspect the thoughts of others. As king, Edmund would by his very nature be distrustful. He would have every reason to see the truth of Iago's famous dictum that

> . . . riches fineless is as poor as winter
> To him that ever fears he shall be poor.

without, however, the humility to regret his choice or to make whatever amendments might insure personal happiness.There is no nostalgia in the life of Edmund, no reveries about happier days. The past means nothing to him. He is driven onward by an egotistical sense of advancement to a future when he will have o'er leapt all boundaries that did seem to contain him and will stand supreme in the midst of his own accomplishments. It is perhaps as fortunate for him as for the land he would rule, that his dream never comes true. The fatal sword of an adversary cuts into his flesh at the moment when all seems near fulfillment. Albany alone stands in his way, and who can say how that combat might have gone? Only as Edmund lies dying does he reflect on something other than his dream of power—"Yet Edmund was beloved"—and attempt something virtuous—"Some good I mean to do, despite of mine own nature."

We anticipate too much, no doubt, in attempting to see the full meaning of Edmund's character. As with Lear's reaction to Cordelia and Kent, the underlying significance is not revealed until the course taken has been traveled for some considerable distance. Like Frost's two roads that diverged in a yellow wood, the difference between one and the other appears not so very great at the moment of starting. As there are many who cry down the love test as too insignificant to bring about the terrible results that follow, there are those who see in Edmund's nihilism a rather commonplace rejection of the "system" and close their eyes to what his rejection leads to. Between Edmund and many others who parade sentiments very similar to his a wide difference exists. He *acts* upon the principles he lays down. If we speak with some passion, therefore, of the goals of this opportunist, it is with good reason.

At the time that Edmund first reveals his plans he confronts us with the choice as to whether respect for a venerable personage or office must be constant or whether such respect must depend upon suitability and nothing else. If we envision only sincere and pure-minded people, there may be little to choose between the two; each has its merits and no one would take unfair advantage. But when we apply this choice to life as we find it, the variables and possibilities are so many that we despair of applying so theoretical a principle. However, the very complexities that face us are instructive. The first of these would naturally concern the person in office. How much does he deserve whatever respect he gets? The answer will have some bearing on those who give it. What unusual circumstances might have arisen which, without lessening respect, would urge them to assume control in practical matters? This is the question facing Henry Bolingbroke and his supporters when Richard II has proved to be corrupt and utterly deaf to the voices of reason. The solution appears simple enough at first, but after it is tried complications arise and plague Henry till the day of his death.

On the other hand, suitability is a criterion so difficult to define that almost anyone will have his own definition. Good motives and bad can do with the term as they see fit.

Now, with Gloucester, there is no question of his suitability to continue being Earl or to continue as father to his two sons. The supposed senility of Lear has at least been argued. But Gloucester has committed no such folly as Lear has, yet Edmund perpetrates a monstrous fraud upon him, which is only part of a larger fraud. The justification for doing this is but dimly revealed in the words which Edmund imputes to his brother. The real reason is that all distinctions have no meaning and can therefore be disregarded. Suitability is to be found in the person himself, of whatever rank or no rank at all, whose dimensions are well compact, whose mind is generous and his shape true. This cold rationality of rejection has never been more succinctly appraised than in Hudson's summation of Edmund's character:

> Edmund's strength and acuteness of intellect, unsubjected as they are to the moral and religious sentiments, exempt him from the superstitions that prevail about him. He has an eye to discern the error of such things, but no sense for the deeper truth they involve. For such superstitions are the natural suggestions of the religious instincts unenlightened by Revelation. So that he who would not be superstitious without Revelation would probably be irreligious with it. . . In other words, Edmund is a free-thinker; not in the right philosophical sense of the term, but in the old historic sense; that is, one in whom the intellect owns no allegiance to the conscience. No awe of Duty, no religious fear to do or think wrong, is allowed to repress or abridge his freedom of thought.[16]

The parallel significance of the Lear plot and the Gloucester plot has frequently been noted. What is too often missed is the relationship between Edmund's cosmic view and Lear's, the one so eloquently defended, the other merely assumed. The clash between these divergent views is striking as the two plots move long independently of each other. Because Edmund has forced us to dwell on the matter of "justification," even a specious justification, we see in a new light the meaning of King Lear himself. He does outlive his suitability to be king. What is most clear is that none of those still loyal to him remains so out of any practical consideration. He could not possibly be restored to rule (as he is in the Tate version), and in this departure forever from the office of kingship we have the first glimmerings as to why Shakespeare chose the tragic ending rather than the happy one. What is here dramatized is best aired in a play in which there is no return, no reward, no peaceful resumption of the old order. Good plays may be written in which such things happen and we all get that sense of fulfillment so notably lacking in *King Lear*. It is only in the tragic holocaust, about which so many have complained, that what we begin to sense as early as the first act can attain the sublime dimensions it deserves. Its victory, as we shall see, is not in its success but in its meaning.

IV

AFTERMATH AND PRELUDE

There is a mystical quality in a king who survives his rule, an almost apocalyptic revelation. Speak no evil of the dead. Mark Antony to the contrary, evil is more likely to abide with the living than to continue in a life of its own when they have passed away. Those who are still with us have not yet attained that immateriality whereby their annoying faults have dissolved, while the more abstract man survives in the thoughts of those who disapproved of him when he was alive. Well may Henry 1V say, "And now my death changes the mode." Though Mark Antony must have sincerely felt from the beginning that Brutus was "the noblest Roman of them all," he could not have so feelingly contradicted his earlier maxim but that the lifeless body of his adversary plucks it out of him. Even the swaggering Coriolanus by his death turns the hatred of Aufidius to something like reverence:

> Though in this city he
> Hath widowed and unchilded many a one
> Which to this hour bewail the injury,
> Yet he shall have a noble memory.

Richard II was murdered and came eventually to be a martyr and a "sweet lovely rose" to the very ones who assisted in his overthrow. But Lear lives. Despite the fact that he did not foresee the anomalous position in which he would find himself, his reign is now history. Yet he still comes and goes, inspiring is some the respect usually bestowed upon the deceased, and in others a distaste for the troublesome old man "that still would manage those authorities that he hath given away."

It were too simple a thesis to defend Lear purely on the strength of these two attitudes and compile two lists of characters: those who honor him and those who do not. I do not mean that the point is trivial; I mean that it is altogether too obvious. In the steadfastness of Kent, Cordelia, Edgar, Gloucester and Albany, and again in the treachery of Goneril, Regan, Cornwall, Edmund and Oswald, the case is overwhelmingly in favor of Lear. There should be no doubt about it. However, misconceptions are sometimes carried into theatrical performances, and the stage "business" — with what seems like textual justification — permits actions which have a very professional look on the boards (as opposed to the "amateur" look: actors just walk on and give their lines) but are quite out of keeping with the story of the play.

A case in point is the portrayal of Lear and his knights in the way Goneril describes them:

> Men so disordered, so deboshed and bold,
> That this our Court, infected with their manners,
> Shows like a riotous inn. Epicurism and lust
> Make it more like a tavern or a brothel
> Than a graced palace.

There needs no scholar come with documents in hand to tell us of wine-drinking kings of yore. Many a royal court has, I dare say, appeared "more like a tavern or a brothel than a graced palace." But Goneril's words suggest that any such behavior is considerably out of fashion. Lear stoutly denies that his knights are anything but "men of choice and rarest parts, that all particulars of duty know." The only knight who has any lines in the play gives no indication of anything but soft-spoken respectability.

Albany has no idea how the quarrel began between Goneril and her father, though if the knights' behavior were only half as bad as she says it is, he could not help suspecting. Shakespeare wrote no scene in which riotous behavior takes place, nor any scene in which it is conveyed through sound effects from off stage.[17]

It is sometimes true, unfortunately, that when an uncongenial situation exists we must seek some pretext for bringing it to a head, or, as Goneril puts it, we must "breed from hence occasions." But there is no need in this case, if we may safely judge from her complaints. The catalogue of woes, which she recites to Oswald, would lead us to believe that things have reached an intolerable pass, and just why she must contrive additional reasons for having it "come to question" is anything but clear.

It is significant the number of those who quote Goneril and Regan to substantiate their reading of Lear as testy, choleric, overbearing, etc. The conversation between these two includes such phrases as "the infirmity of his age," "hath ever but slenderly known himself," "imperfections of long-ingrafted condition," "unruly waywardness," "infirm and choleric years." Since they are talking together in private, many see no reason to doubt what they say, unlike their public avowals of love which are patently false, and for a rather evident purpose. When Goneril complains of her father wronging her by day and night she is talking with her steward, and since the conversation is again a private one, the tendency is to accept what she says as true, the idea evidently being that private talks are always truthful—unless we can show that Goneril has some motive to fool Regan or Regan to fool Goneril, or again that Goneril would want to deceive Oswald.

The character of Goneril is just beginning to emerge with some clarity, and what strikes us first is her assertive way of proclaiming things that are strangely unsubstantiated by anything specific. Her father struck her gentleman for chiding of the fool. The fool, we learn a little later, is "all-licensed," this charge occasioned by his remark that Lear was a pretty fellow when he had no need to care for his daughter's frowning. And when Lear sarcastically asks Goneril, "Your name, fair gentle-woman?" she replies that this admiration (i.e., pretended amazement) is much o' the savor of his other new pranks. None of these things is in any way comparable to the "gross crimes" which happen, according to her, "by day and night," and "every hour." Yet she takes each one and flourishes it as if it were typical of the terrible things she must endure. Lear's striking her gentleman starts her off: "By day and night he wrongs me." She mentions the "all-licensed fool" as if he were part and parcel of the disorderly group shaking the very peace of her castle:

> Not only, sir, this your all-licensed fool,
> But other of your insolent retinue
> Do hourly carp and quarrel . . .

And her father's pretended astonishment as to who this grand lady might be is "much o' the savor . . ."

The apparent forthrightness with which Goneril speaks is a revelation of her character, her manner, her psychology, and not a disclosure of facts about which we would otherwise be ignorant. Her resplendent beauty—as I picture her—her open insolence, her grand manner lend a cater-gorical finality to anything she says. We can almost admire the effect she creates, yet hate her with good reason. To see her and hear her is to recognize immediately the kind of royalty *she* is, a type that extends to older offspring of high-placed families, and her actions from this scene onward confirm our first impression.

Thus do we find Goneril imperious rather than energetic. She is not the conscious liar that Edmund is. She does not openly acknowledge to herself that what she says is untrue yet that she will pretend it *is* true in order to gain something for herself. Edmund is shown actually plotting to tell lies to his father. We never see Goneril doing so. Her brief conversation with Regan toward the close of the first scene concerns a plan to act upon what she has already concluded is so. It has nothing to do with avowed deceit.

Goneril has that all-engulfing selfishness which interprets the world about her according to her own moods. The sight of a handsome young man excites her craving to possess him, regardless of the fact that she has an honorable and devoted husband. She does not speak of lust, not even in terms of the attractions of illicit love or her own defiance of the laws relating to the marriage contract. No. It is an *honorable* step with her:

> My fool usurps my body.

The "fool," of course, is not simply lacking in romantic appeal; he lacks, if we are to believe Goneril, masculine firmness in the time of crisis:

> It is the cowish terror of his spirit,
> That dares not undertake. He'll not feel wrongs
> Which tie him to an answer.

As the crisis grows, the reasons for Albany's hesitancy in acting are made quite plain and, whether we consider them adequate or not, they have nothing whatever to do with that "cowish terror" which simply serves as an excuse for Goneril's lust.

Such people as she are capable of conscious falsehood but they resort to it only when it is forced upon them. They do not, as a rule, sit quietly deliberating the lies they will tell. It is Goneril's temperament rather than her ambition that drives her. Her father grates upon her.

THE ROYALTY OF LEAR

Consequently her self-righteousness causes her not merely to say but actually to think:

> By day and night he wrongs me.

She does not speak in soliloquy, as Edmund does, but complains to her steward Oswald, who performs the role so necessary to people of her stamp: "a bawd in the way of good service." Oswald will agree with every word his mistress says.

In a sense it is true that her allegations come first and the refutation comes afterward. However, we are not totally unprepared to suspect Goneril. The closing lines of the first scene indicated a plan that she and her sister would put into effect as a means of guarding against the King's dangerous moods. The fact that we do not know precisely what it will be forces us to regard her more closely for any subterfuge she may be practicing. Furthermore mistaken impressions can be guarded against by the actress who performs the role, provided she does so in the haughty, overriding manner of one accustomed to having her own way once she is safely ensconced in power. We should be prepared, therefore, for an obvious contradiction between what she speaks so brazenly here and what she says later to her husband:

> A hundred knights!
> 'Tis politic and safe to let him keep
> At point a hundred knights. Yes, that on every dream,
> Each buzz, each fancy, each complaint, dislike,
> He may enguard his dotage with their powers
> And hold our lives in mercy.

This is spoken in mild sarcasm, as if it were a truth as plain as day, yet it is hardly a story of "rank and not to be endured riots" or "deboshed knights," supposedly the things she can no longer endure. Rather it tells of a danger, or at least a pretended danger, that Lear's armed followers stand ready to defend his troublesome dotage.

We need not relate in exhausting detail all the little facts that refute Goneril, though they are many. Her personality is the center of interest here, an unrestrained and emotional selfishness that sees life according to its pleasure and displeasure and affixes right or wrong accordingly. She is a tempestuous beauty, magisterial, disdainful of the opposition she can ignore, furious at the annoyances she cannot. The confrontation with her father has all the appearance of righteous wrath; her talk later with her husband is equally righteous, though in a softer tone. We wonder how a person can be so unabashed in her manner and so contradictory in what she says. But these shifts are consistent with her and are made far plainer than any of the "truths" she flaunts so openly.

Not essentially a plotter, Goneril is astute enough to take advantage of an opportunity presented her. The love test is served up to her, and she accordingly responds with flattery. Her scheme for the murder of her husband is a rather obvious way of getting rid of him so that she may enjoy her lover, nor does she seem to have any precautions in mind lest the finger of suspicion point at her. Edmund's machinations are much more carefully thought out, so much so that not only does he ruin people that stand in his way but he takes care that his reputation is actually enhanced in the process. Consequently, we may say that he profits by his sharp perception of good and evil. Though he scoffs at the moral significance of either one, he is not indifferent to their effect on others. Goneril's self-righteousness, on the other hand, is blind to the practical need for deception, and she comes right out and falsely accuses her father to his face. The contradictory story she later gives her husband, since it is no more than a shift for quite obvious reasons, hardly suggests a delibera- tive mentality. She feigns no regrets over what has just taken place. She seems utterly unaware of the discrepancy between the cold indifference with which she watches her father storm out of the palace and her public declaration in the first scene that her love for him was such as "makes breath poor and speech unable." Were it pointed out to her she would undoubtedly make one of her characteristic responses: "Pray you, content," or "No more, the text is foolish." Since her father is an annoyance to her, the measure of her resentment must be found in his deeds. Consequently he and his knights flash into one gross crime or other. The process, painfully spelled out, is in Goneril's mind an immediate reflex, evil women being as intuitive toward what they must pretend to be true as good women are toward what they know to be true.

Goneril is incapable of enjoying what she possesses. She knows only the irritation that, one way or another, will always attend it. Her first thought, after she has been granted her half of the kingdom, is the problem her father will turn out to be; a small price for a person whose expectations are much humbler, for her it is much too high. In the royal atmosphere in which she has been raised a nature such as hers is apt to go undetected till it assumes full power. On the surface she may appear to be not unlike Lear himself in her facile adaptation to court life. Like him she undoubtedly has that in her countenance that subjects would fain call master, and if Lear sees in her an image of himself, it is not necessarily the blindness or the egotism of a parent that permits him to see nothing else. She was born to rule but not to love. The second disqualifies her from the first. Only when she assumes the position of rule does it become apparent that she is incapable of those sacrifices, often little ones, which love entails and which must be given freely. In response to a professed love, for which we would imagine no sacrifice would be too great, she was granted all she now possesses. Between her and her father, so alike in demeanor and so different at heart, we await the inevitable clash.

The movement of *The Tragedy of King Lear* is like that of a musical masterpiece. We must be attuned to its power, its soft sweetness, its temporary interludes, its magnificent climaxes. Had the play been written without careful attention to these structural variations, it would undoubtedly have been an excellent play of character and story, but even these are more deeply impressed by the manner in which they are presented.

The dramatic outburst of the opening scene passes and the action comes, almost as a natural course, to a quieter and easier tempo, the tearful farewell of Cordelia the last expression of emotion. Even this is done in very gentle accents. The stage, crowded and colorful a few moments ago, becomes practically deserted. Goneril and Regan talk quietly to each other. Their conversation is matter-of-fact. The contrast between what they say now and the love that they avowed previously is not nearly so marked as their change of tone. Not that they were particularly emotional when their father called upon them to speak. But there was a formality to their words, a quality of *recitative,* an undeniable elocution by which we differentiate public speech from private. In their very naturalness now we can infer more pointedly an artificiality in what they said before. The casual way in which the avowals of love are ignored as they turn to the practical matter of wielding that power which public oratory has secured for them is most striking. The new order is beginning to emerge—in subdued tones and in private.

Edmund appears—by himself. His soliloquy to Nature, like the conversation between Goneril and Regan, is calm. Brutal and terrifying in substance, it is not delivered with passion. No one was ever more self-possessed than Edmund as he senses that the times have become opportune. He needs no emotional superlatives to rally a reluctant spirit. He is not angry. His illegitimate birth he can henceforth disregard. The time has come when distinctions between legitimate and illegitimate, older brother and younger, will no longer apply.

The effect of this slowing of the action and limiting stage appearances to no more than two over a stretch of some 261 lines—through the beginning of Scene iv, in which Kent appears by himself—is that of a sombre passage of music, deeply intoned yet softly played, a cool deliberate kind which is both aftermath and prelude. Voices that we heard a short while before, brief and reverent, sound now in another key. It is as if the orchestra had begun the work with a theme that was stately at the very commencement, formal and compliant to our expectations of what the development was to be, only to have a tempestuous outburst take over—one soft instrument sustaining itself the while, and finally trailing off after the orchestra has returned to its original stateliness. We now have a resumption of some of those instruments that sounded in the first part. Both tone and theme are new. All else is quiet. Curiously, the theme is ominous but not discordant. It may be that the climactic uproar in that opening scene has given all smoother sounds a contrasting kind of harmony.

The effect is a heightening of what we must almost strain to catch. The raging mistakes of the righteous are the opportunities of the stealthy unrighteous. When true authority undermines itself, the self-seeking and the ambitious have their advantage. The stormy passion of Lear, the unimpassioned cunning of Edmund, follow in a very natural kind of sequence, and he who can act so openly is blind where he who acts in covert is perceptive. Even the tricking of Old Gloucester is tranquil compared with its parallel action in the opening scene, yet how crystal clear the means and the purpose to which it is directed.

We may pause here for a moment to note that such

psychological development and such careful management of the dramatic atmosphere would be impossible if intruded upon by a drunken and disorderly rout, sometimes staged, sometimes imagined, absolutely unjustified by anything in the text: knights singing and bellowing drunkenly, wine cups held at a tipsy angle and spilling over tables, chairs and floor, furniture being smashed, servants slapped and tossed about. No such thing happens. There is an unbroken stillness about the play, in both the castle of Gloucester and the palace of the Duke of Albany, as perfidy goes quietly about its work. The only intrusion upon this stillness is the blast of the hunting horn, which has all the heartiness of a return home after the day's hunt, just as Lear's first words are hearty, rugged and completely unsuspicious of the sinister plot awaiting him:

Let me not stay a jot for dinner. Go get it ready.

It is difficult to say precisely what has taken place between Scenes i and iii. We are sure that Lear has not forgotten Cordelia for a single moment. She must ever loom up in his thoughts, try as he will to keep her out. Alternately his conscience upsets him and then is wrenched to justify his treatment of the daughter he loved most. If he were wrong he has treated her most foully; if he were right, *she* treated *him* so. Either way, a deep affection was wronged. Conscience is only one part of him that is upset. His entire soul is in constant torment, as first one side is turned to the flame and then the other in a desperate attempt to find relief as the pain becomes unbearable. Any love that Goneril has to offer serves but to emphasize the love he threw away, but it is doubtful that he can bear to look upon her in this way. Only his suffering is real.

We can presume such a Lear, and the text is not lacking in hints that would seem to put him in that light. With some curiosity we look forward to his re-entry on

stage, particularly to see if Goneril's complaints have some
basis in the wound from which he suffers. Perhaps he is
just a little short-tempered on occasion, as might be noted
for instance when he cuts off the knight's mention of
Cordelia going to France:

> No more of that . . .

What we see, however, is not a wounded or a suffering
king, but a man of sound constitution and right good
appetite, and showing no signs whatever of moodiness or
depression.

The effect is a curious one. A fleeting impression that
he has banished Cordelia from his thoughts as well as from
his presence gives way to the more probable explanation:
Lear is in perfect command of himself. Without denying
the anguish we assume him to be undergoing, without even
mitigating it in the smallest degree, we must acknowledge
that he is king over it. Certainly he does not flash into one
gross crime or other, even as a way of venting the pent-up
emotion he feels. Lear is not a man to brood. What he has
inflicted on Cordelia he has, in a sense, inflicted on himself
as well. He will bear with it. Strength, not weakness, is
what lends passion to his eventual downfall and creates the
soul-stirring sympathy in those who remain loyal to him.

It is at this moment that he is greeted by the disguised
Kent, who gives his reason for wanting to be in Lear's
service:

> . . . you have that in your countenance which
> I would fain call master.
>> LEAR. What's that?
>> KENT. Authority.

The absurdity of Kent saying this to a senile king whose
wits have begun to turn, or to an intemperate guilt-

ridden father, or yet again to a dissipated reveler — is too obvious to need comment. Nor are Kent's words part of a disguise or a means of insinuating himself into the King's good graces. He would not flatter before nor does he do it now. What he says is much like what he said in the opening scene:

> Royal Lear,
> Whom I have ever honored as my King,
> Loved as my father, as my master followed ...

minus any identifying tags of previous association.

The contrast between Kent's "master" and Goneril's "idle old man" is so glaring as to permit no compromise between the two. No matter how we analyze either statement, we can get no more meaning out of what is so plainly put. The college sophomore who sees the question here as a simple matter of which one he will believe, Goneril or Kent, has the message just as surely as the scholar steeped in his researches. There was no "idle old man" in the first scene, nor is there evidence of any in the thirty-five lines of conversation between Lear and Kent, nor again in the twenty-nine lines of further talk with the knight. Taken together these two conversations are of sufficient length, as poetic drama goes, to indicate some signs of what Goneril's bitter complaints might have led us to expect. Lear's irascibility with Oswald, if not a perfect specimen of forbearance, is not inconsistent with Kent's "master," and is partly the result of the great abatement of kindness which the knight has noticed and partly the result of Oswald's insolence.

In this scene Lear is away from the throne and all courtly magnificence. We see him in as unregal a situation as we could find for one who is still king and still accustomed to obedience and respect. His language throughout, till the rupture with Goneril, is cast in the prose of subjects less exalted than those the kingly office is wont to concern itself with and has a robust vigor to it. Even his jocular remark to Kent—

> If thou be as poor for a subject as he is for a king, thou art poor enough—

is the kind of humor a person of higher rank might use upon himself, provided he has a sense of humor. Strong, rugged, hearty—this is the man, just as that august figure in the opening scene is the king. To this man comes the disguised Kent and reasserts his respect for authority at a time that the man who represents it holds the title and very little else. It is the countenance of Lear that inspires this respect, not what he continues to hold by virtue of office. Kent's love runs deep and, though he condemns and approves according to laws by which king and servant are bound alike, his love is never so impersonal as to cease the moment these laws are transgressed. A dog may be obeyed in office, and so may a mountebank. But the man cannot be so separated from his position that the pretender is respected in it and the true man ignored out of it.

The meeting of these two is symbolic. What Kent says now is as much in character as his previous defiance of the King:

> I can keep honest counsel, ride, run, mar a curious tale in telling it, and deliver a plain message bluntly. That which ordinary men are fit for, I am qualified in, and the best of me is diligence.

The man who professes "to love him that is honest" is the same man who calls Oswald the son and heir of a mongrel bitch. The name is concealed, the accents are borrowed, the likeness is razed. But Lear sees the true Kent under the guise of a stranger and likes him. Though Kent pretends not to know who Lear is, we can believe that his reason for service is the authority Lear has in his countenance. The concealment that Kent practices has no dishonest purpose nor does he resort to any untruthfulness as part of his disguise. Man faces man and the attraction is mutual—a fitting prelude to the appearance of Goneril and the petty dislikes with which she makes "cause" for the tender of a wholesome weal.

Interpreted thus, the rupture between Goneril and Lear has dramatic significance that simply cannot be matched by the story of a superannuated father or a king whose troublesome habits are a source of annoyance to those about him. Goneril's accusations and Lear's replies are plain enough—who could possibly misread them? Even the emotion with which they are spoken is difficult to miss as we go over the printed page. But what a tremendous difference it makes how we interpret—and consequently portray on the stage—the two principle actors! To degrade the father-king into anything like the pitiful figure which Lamb rejected, or to justify the daughter as rightly incensed over her father's misbehavior, all evidence of the play to the contrary, and then to offer these two meager characters as figures of high tragedy!

It is through such misreading that the play has been criticized for having the climax in the first scene with all else aftermath. A daughter trying to talk some sense into her carousing father, who in turn becomes enraged and leaves her house—such a story is not without pathos or even some social value as regards care of the aged, but this is not what happens in *King Lear* nor could it conceivably have any relationship to the grandeur of the action that follows.

The subtlety of Shakespearean presentation transcends the weight of verbiage and oftentimes the beauties of poetry itself. A single line or two in very plain English takes on the significance of the character who speaks it and the intensity of the situation to which it relates. The few words Kent says to his master have the force of a dramatic soliloquy, which a lesser dramatist would have been sorely tempted to employ at this point. It is enough that we recognize Kent in his disguise and listen for the reason of his return to this King who is on the point of being forced to quit his daughter's home. Brevity is best. Goneril is quite expansive in her enumeration of the King's faults, as expansive as she was when professing her great love for him, and is false on each occasion. Kent's few words are sincere. Between the two we must make our choice. Like the bond according to which Cordelia loves, nor more nor less, Kent's words may appear unimpressive when matched against more detailed eloquence, but we are at a great turning point in the play and have by this time learned to see a deeper significance in truths bluntly uttered, as opposed to falsehoods spoken with great elaboration.

It is through Kent, not Goneril, that we see Lear at this moment. A king who has committed the folly Lear has may be open to various interpretations. The most outspoken critic of that folly is the one whose convictions we cannot ignore, either when he praises or when he condemns his master.

Through Kent, says Bradley,[18] we see Lear in his prime. Unquestionably we do, but we see the present Lear as well, and we should be very careful about implications in the expression "Lear in his prime." Does it imply a Lear quite different from the one we see now? Is Kent no more than a personalized kind of nostalgia for the past, or again an indication of the honor Lear once deserved but deserves no longer? I am sure Bradley did not intend quite this much, but even the least impression if it be the wrong one obscures the truth. I am not saying that age has made no difference at all, in the way that Bradley evidently means, but simply that this difference is unimportant when we consider all the evidence for the robust health of Lear, and that his great age, since it does not incapacitate him in any way, renders him a more august figure than the younger Lear in the prime of life. "You have that in your countenance. . ." Kent speaks in the present tense: "You *have,* not "You *once had."* He could hardly do other, some might object. True, but he had done better to avoid this altogether if there be no truth in it, instead of flattering a man who—Lear's senility again!—has Prufrockian sensitivities about signs of age.

To consider the source of unflattering notions of Lear that have gained much acceptance in scholarly commentary is itself too simple. The source must be analyzed. Goneril's filial relationship enables her to take liberties another subject would blush to think about, and thereby perverts the cermonious affection to which a king far less revered than Lear would be entitled. Kinship is, to her, intimacy without love. She has an eye for the faults of those nearest her, we might almost say a psychological need to condemn in order to explain away her perpetual dissatisfaction with life. Boredom is a chronic affliction with her, to a degree that makes a well-balanced life virtually impossible. Such people have been known to hate the very walls of the houses in which they live. We may well wonder whether some Freudian transference of guilt might not account for her fiction about Lear and his knights hourly carping and quarreling and breaking forth in not to be endured riots, since, if anyone in the play has a mad impulse to smash furniture and mistreat servants, it would be Goneril.

Perhaps I exaggerate slightly in probing her mind. The error would be one of degree, however, rather than of kind. Her type is clearly set forth in all the little episodes and conversations, and we find it quite in her character to loathe her father, despise her husband, and come eventually into an unholy rivalry with her sister—the one with whom she once planned to "hit together"—and poison her. I do not believe that Goneril is a particularly sensual person, as some have thought her to be because of her illicit love for Edmund. She is simply an unhappy person. Fierce in her condemnation of those about her, she has a roving eye for someone at a remove. Surely such a daughter is an unreliable witness as to her father's faults.

As the father-daughter bond came, somewhat unfittingly, into the first scene, it takes over the present one completely, in its strangely perverted way. Through her very ties to her father Goneril sees him as nothing more than an "idle old man." Kinship without love! To her this is all in all. Since she has spoken first, we anticipate the confrontation that follows, purely as a matter between Lear and his eldest daughter, and we may be just a little too carried away by the pathos of it. What happens, however, involves the King as well as the father. If the reception is unfit and the rupture appalling, the royal personage is not annihilated by family ties, though the daughter is corrupted by them.

The Lear who is about to be cast off is a grand figure, nothing less. Kent, straightforward under all circumstances, tells us this. The scene we are going to witness will tell us so again. Only the most rigid attention to the most careful dramatic preparation can make us receptive to a calamity as grand and impressive as the man who suffers it.

V

THE FOOL

Though the fool is young, as all evidence suggests, we may suppose an association between him and his master that has extended back over some period of time, and not devoid of affection on both sides. If the fool has been in court long enough to have a deep liking for Cordelia, deep enough to cause him great sorrow over her going to France, we can assume that he has been with his master long before the division of the kingdom was even contemplated. Expositor of Lear's folly, the fool has justly commanded attention. Neither in what he says, however, nor in his manner of saying it does he give us any evidence to suggest that Lear has been a selfish authoritarian accustomed to being flattered.

This strangely assorted pair, for all the long connection between kings and fools in history and in story, produces an effect which is utterly lost if we accept Lear and his fool as a purely conventional arrangement so often seen as to present no novelty now. Undoubtedly their association has been a very normal thing in the past, the fool's barbs being a source of amusement to King and court alike, as is evidenced by Lear's calling for him several times before he makes his appearance. To imagine that the fool has always been what he turns out to be in the play—a stinging reminder of his master's foolishness—makes as little sense as to imagine the fool has been blind to, or forgetful of, the presumed evil of the King's ways in the past, of which the love test is supposed to be a typical example. What Lear's behavior was like over an indeterminate period of time is as plainly suggested by the fool as it is by Cordelia.

The most outstanding characteristic of the fool is his bluntness. Throughout the play his comments will suprise us by the very obviousness of the things he mentions—not unlike the army recruit who points out a colonel's mistake when men of higher rank can think of no tactful way of mentioning it. What is in the minds of everyone may preserve a certain propriety as long as it is not put into words. But the fool continually amazes us with his directness. He reveals nothing that we do not already know ourselves; the mere fact that he says it at all, and to the King's face, is what strikes us. In a fool, though his function permits him just this kind of license, the seriousness of the things on which he comments lends him a perpetual unseemliness, one that we never become accustomed to though we learn to expect it. He blurts out what the more decorous leave unsaid.

Furthermore the fool's chatter, unlike Kent's few brief words, is constant and long, recurring over and over again. Even as we witness the play in performance, we have ample opportunity to reflect upon questions not unlike those I have already posed with respect to Cordelia and her father. Has Lear *always* demanded flattery and subservience? If so, has the fool been the lone exception?—and for what reason? We all recognize with Olivia that

> There is no slander in an allowed fool, though he do nothing but rail . . .

and that a king permits liberties to a fool that he would permit to no one else. But I simply cannot believe that a king who is supposedly arrogant and delights in flattery would allow himself to be publicly "roasted" by his fool

simply because of a time-honored tradition. For such a
Lear it would be a difficult thing indeed, and I cannot help
wondering whether he would have struck Goneril's gentleman "for chiding of his fool."

I do not seriously suggest this possibility, except to
show what is presupposed by persisting theories as to
Lear's overbearing tyranny. The story of this royal
monarch and the fool who attends him is not the
continuation of any such past, as we can easily see by
reading carefully what they do and say. From the moment
the fool enters he makes biting remarks about the King's
disposition of the land and the consequences that have
ensued. This is evidently not what Lear expects when he
calls for him (he calls no fewer than six times). When the
fool begins to make unpleasant references to the daughters, Lear threatens him:

Take heed, sirrah, the whip.

He remarks on the bitterness of what the fool says:

A pestilent gall to me!
A bitter fool!

The King asks him at one point:

Dost thou call me fool, boy?

Surely this is not a typical conversation that took place
many times when the kingdom was undivided and Lear
ruled supreme in the land. The subject is a new and painful
one. Granted that the fool is not essentially different from
what he always was, when he would make blunt remarks
that could prove embarrassing to the one concerned—
doubtless the King bore his share—nevertheless this kind of
wit must have had only the most harmless matter to feed

on. With a character such as the fool, his very sameness is what makes the difference. Nothing can vary so much as blunt foolery on an innocent topic and a tender one.

Lear's mood varies between vexation and pained meditation. He has not had to listen to anything like this before because he has not done anything comparable to the folly about which the fool keeps talking, and if he had, the fool is not one to remain quiet about it. We miss completely the irony of the fool's role if we assume he has always been the "pestilent gall" he proves to be now.

As a character in his own right, the fool deserves no less than to be portrayed faithfully, and this is possible only if we see a brand of humor that switches from the typical subjects of a well-regulated royal court, "flashes of merriment that were wont to set the table on a roar," to a new and decidedly anomalous situation. As with others in the play, however, a correct interpretation of the fool depends largely on a correct interpretation of Lear himself. Projecting Lear backward on the basis of what happens in the opening scene, we tend to—indeed we *must*—project the fool on the same basis. This would appear, on the surface, to simplify the story, but it involves so much that is unlikely that we must discard it altogether.

The fool may indeed give to Lear the first glimmerings of how wrong was the treatment of Cordelia, and Lear, moody and thoughtful under the impact, finds the fool more difficult to stifle than the knight. Plain common sense has found a persistent voice. Simple truth is all on the side of the fool. In his heart Lear must concede this, as his replies strongly suggest. But even this much is certainly to the King's credit, and if it does not in itself make him a towering ideal it is certainly inconsistent with the idea of an overbearing or witless Lear living upon the flattery of those beneath him. Truth is often more tactless than a lie. False accusations have not the power to injure one's *amour-propre* that the true have, and Lear shows a certain honesty of mind in remaining passive under the attacks of the fool while raging back at the lies of Goneril and the insolence of Oswald. Somewhere in Lear common sense responds, painfully, to the common sense of the fool. This is much in a king who, we might imagine, would be easily tempted to justify everything he does, particularly those public mistakes that compromise the royal image.

Keats has said, "The fool's words are merely the simplest translation of poetry as high as Lear's. The fool gives a finishing touch to the pathos."[19] There is considerable merit in this so long as we understand that the translation is not for the sake of clarity. Whatever thoughts Lear may have at this point are more effective if left unspoken in the mysteries of his mind. If we try to imagine what he is thinking, though we could never be certain, we are actively expressing a kind of sympathy in making the attempt. Sometimes the strongest concern for another comes in the form of seeking to know rather than actually knowing. If put into words, Lear's meditations would require the subtleties of high poetry. But it is contrary to the character of Lear to speak them. His peremptory "No more of that" shows the sensitivity of a strong man to what threatens, if pursued far enough, to unman him, or at least to mar what he stands for in the eyes of his people. It is better that he remain as we see him, those tender emotions of the heart concealed under a tough exterior and no more than hinted through brief responses to the artless candor of someone else.

While the fool does not mention Cordelia, his much pining away at her departure—the first mention of that unhappy event—is the source of his remarks and reveals a kind of identity between what he says and what his master refuses to say. Cordelia has gone out of their lives. Goneril and Regan are now in power. It is the first of these that brings the fool's attention to the second. It is the second that will cause Lear to reflect on the first:

> O most small fault,
> How ugly didst thou in Cordelia show!

In these opposite workings of the mind we see the difference between him who rules and him who does not. Decision belongs to the office of kingship: a wrong one is more kingly than none at all. We may argue the point, yet feel in our hearts that honest doubt and proper meekness are not the qualities we look for in a ruler. If he decides wrongly, we are called upon to criticize his error, but if he cannot make up his mind, we feel that frustration of being confronted with nothing, either good or bad. Plato's insistence that kings should be philosophers and philosophers kings is a true ideal which life as we find it can aspire to but is not likely to reach in even the most perfect society. In the thinker we honor hesitation, but we demand decisiveness in those who hold political office.

It is this unavoidable quality that is perhaps at war with the tenderer feelings in Lear. What we are quick to call pride may be simply the practice of what has long been a virtue in one who has borne on his shoulders the heavy responsibilities of a nation's government. Is Lear really to blame for being accustomed to having his own way? Have not others been as set on his having it as ever he himself was? The royal prerogative is a duty as well as an indulgence. Consequently, when Lear banished his best-loved daughter and his most faithful follower, he was using that power of command he had so often used in the past. Wrong? Yes, terribly wrong, but who can fix such guilt with any precision? The psychology of power, if we make an exception of out-and-out cruelty, begets very understandable tendencies that are conveniently absent in lesser men. Manner oftentimes determines matter. The least we can do is understand this.

Those of us who have never had the responsibility of high command will feel a natural affinity with the fool, whose barbs cut through all the complications of office, of which insolence is only the most apparent. The real Lear is at a remove from our simpler and homelier views of life. The false Lear we dismiss as arrogant, proud and selfish. But the fool, even partially demented as he may be, is completely unfettered, almost pure in his perception of reality. He is a violation, yet perfectly right in what he says. The clash between this kind of truth and something else that is essentially good (a *bad* Lear is simply a convenient way out of the paradox) becomes a pathway to perfection, a purging of what we might call the almost necessary evils of authority. Common sense points them out, but, though we commend what we hear we can never so simplify our view as to make the fool a chorus for the play.

Those closer in rank to the great ones of this world, those who in a sense share some of the status and understand it better are aware of the difficulty of taking remedial action or even speaking aloud. The bluntness of Kent is very different from that of the fool. He who is far removed can be blunt indeed and speak from the blessed simplicity of his own private feelings. But status involves natural reserve and attendance to those proprieties that lesser men know not of. Plain facts belong to the world of those who see nothing else, and in blockheadedness there is a simple, even a very desirable kind of truth. We need not trace the extremes to which such an attitude may lead. Simplicity of this sort may, if given the chance, ride roughshod over the unavoidable intricacies of life and eventually do violence to itself. The argument of simple truth may be cited by the devil to suit his purpose, just as easily as the argument that the king can do no wrong. The fool—and we bless him for it!—is not evil. But this complicates rather than simplifies the outspokenness we love to quote.

It must be confessed that even Goneril realizes

something of all this, in spite of her affectation of forthrightness and in spite of the fact that she now wields the power that once belonged to her father. The "all-licensed fool" is more of a pestilent gall to her than he is to the King, not simply because he reveals what she is — and her sins are worse than Lear's folly — but because his manner is so different from the "discreet proceeding" by which she must gloss over her own purposes. Not scrupling to expose herself by accusations that are far from true, nor yet to making plain her desires, she must first provoke her father to actions that will give her a semblance of rectitude. It is, as I have already stated, Goneril's psychological need of being always in the right that colors her actions. But "being in the right" must suit the occasion, and a daughter scolding her father-king must naturally assume a virtuous reluctance to take on an unpleasant duty:

> . . . the fault
> Would not 'scape censure, nor the redresses sleep,
> Which, in the tender of a wholesome weal,
> Might in their working do you that offense
> Which else were shame, that then necessity
> Will call discreet proceeding.

In Goneril, who is by no means a subtle person, we see that attention to the subtleties of office that is like a return to normalcy after the violations of the fool. With her entry a certain decorum is restored, partly at least because of her resplendent beauty and haughty dignity. What follows is, I think, one of the most interesting and significant parts of the entire play. During this confrontation between Lear and Goneril the fool is present and is continually making remarks. Yet he is ignored. It is as if no one on stage is aware of his presence, and *we* are the only ones to overhear his commentary, inserted deftly into the unbroken dialogue of the other two. As Goneril concludes her catalogue of Lear's misdoings, from which she requests him to desist, the fool offers his own interpretation of what she really intends:

> For, you know, Nuncle,
> "The hedge sparrow fed the cuckoo so long
> That it had it head bit off by it young."
> So out went the candle, and we were left darkling.
>   LEAR. Are you our daughter?
>   GON. Come, sir,
> I would you would make use of that good wisdom
> Whereof I know you are fraught, and put away
> These dispositions that of late transform you
> From what you rightly are.
>   FOOL. May not an ass know when the cart draws the horse?
> Whoop, Jug! I love thee.
>   LEAR. Doth any here know me? This is not Lear.
> Doth Lear walk thus? Speak thus? Where are his eyes?
> Either his notion weakens, his discernings
> Are lethargied—Ha! Waking? 'Tis not so.
> Who is it that can tell me who I am?
>   FOOL. Lear's shadow.
>   LEAR. I would learn that, for, by the marks of sovereignty,
> knowledge, and reason, I should be false persuaded
>   I had daughters.
>   FOOL. Which they will make an obedient father.
>   LEAR. Your name, fair gentlewoman?
>   GON. This admiration, sir, is much o' the savor
> Of other your new pranks. . . .

Goneril accuses her father. His reaction is one of disbelief. The fool is knowing—he rises to new heights. It is apt, for once, that the strangeness of the fool's garb strike a modern audience as bizarre. What we lose in our lack of reverence for kingship and the unbelievable strangeness of the demented fool enlightening the wise king we gain in the alien look of the fool.[20] That which is comical must be familiar—classical figures of comedy are mere curiosities till they can be identified as in some way typical of comedy as we know it today. It is enough that we know Falstaff to be fat, sinful and witty, and to tell remarkable lies about his prowess. For the rest, Falstaffian costume detracts from his comedy, till the familiar transcends the exotic. The fool in *Lear* has been a comical entertainer, but from the moment he steps before us his humor serves quite another purpose. I imagine him as looking very strange and out of place here, and creating an impression much more outlandish than Touchstone did when Jaques met him in the forest.

Beauty, Authority, and something grotesque between them! All three must be what they truly represent. Let not a certain naturalness obscure the fantastic: two members of the same family when they are engaged in a hot dispute, and becoming more and more acrimonious, are likely to ignore the interruptions of a third person and direct their attention wholly toward each other. The lower status of the fool, for all his license to speak freely, would place him outside the circle of a fracas between two people of royal blood. Goneril would not deign to notice the fool; Lear is too dumbfounded by his daughter's attack to mind anything else. Yet we hear all perfectly.

The effect would not be at all the same if the third speaker were one whose license to speak came of a higher station and enabled him to participate on a level closer to that of the King and his daughter. Once reading the scene as we have it from the pen of Shakespeare we are very much aware of the effect it creates. The fool says nothing that is not implicit in the exchange of angry words. Attendant imp, smirking devil, a gargoyle given the power to speak, the fool need not be physically unattractive—and unquestionably he is not—to spread an aura of unreality over what is taking place. To Lear it all has the spell of a weird dream, and the fool furthers the impression as we look on and share the dream with Lear. Can this be

Goneril actually talking so to him? "This is not Lear." The King is more disposed to doubt his own identity than to admit that of a daughter who could treat him thus.

A sentimental portrayal of Lear's feelings would be somewhat out of character at this point and decidedly less effective. "Degenerate bastard!" he thunders at Goneril. Whether the epithet be thought excessive, it is characteristic of a strong and powerful Lear rather than an old man whimpering over his daughter's cruelty. The tears that come to his eyes dishonor him more than the knowledge that he has begotten such a daughter:

> Life and death! I am ashamed
> That thou hast power to shake my mandhood thus,
> That these hot tears, which break from me perforce,
> Should make thee worth them.

There will be sentiment and there will be a weakened Lear as the play goes on. But right now we see a contention between two strong-willed people, and Goneril's victory is not due to any weakness in her father but to the foolish arrangement he made when he resigned his kingly sway and turned it over to her and Regan. His rage is the rage of helpless strength. The unreality of what is made clear to him is the predominant tone, not the pathos of it, and it is the fool that makes this tone not only possible but poetically effective.

The fool's comments are poignant. They lay bare the true character of Goneril as well as the folly of Lear. The clash between the fool's simple truthfulness on the one hand and the more exalted manner of Lear and Goneril on the other is stressed in the language of all three and should be carried out by antic gestures and grimaces as the fool injects his comments.[21]

The remarks themselves as we read them on the printed page are common sense without the vehicle, and mere simplicity is not enough of a contrast to achieve the remarkable effect. Were simplicity all, we would be almost correct in dismissing the decorum of royalty as nonsense and in seeing elemental wisdom as the truth that really matters behind facades of punctiliousness. But the fool, if anything at all, is a defender of the very thing we would be thereby dismissing. He is a violation of the new order, which in turn is a violation of the old. What royal Lear has done to himself and what those others are whom he has set up as his masters are the subject on which the fool comments—not royalty itself, but the desecration of royalty by its own act. The resulting conflict will be fought on a higher level, at which the most deplorable ingratitude will address the King in terms of respect, even when depriving him of his train and driving him into exile. No simple-hearted rustic moralizing over this could go to the heart of the matter as the fool does with his antics, his quips and snatches of song. No character of any description could behave according to his type yet perform such a novel function in the altered state of things.

The hypocrisy by which the dishonest must proceed and the tact by which the honest must speak are alike an indication of the one thing. To all such, the fool comes like a blunt affirmation. He wears his foolery in such a visible manner that to comment or condemn is to become his victim. Like Lear himself, we are compelled to listen in silence. Grudgingly or enthusiastically, we concur in Kent's opinion:

This is not altogether fool, my lord.

In his complexly simply role the fool could not be nearly so effective if he were talking to a mere outcast who had ceased to radiate royal authority. Something of the grandeur of Lear, as we saw it in the opening scene, still impresses us as we see him now with Kent and the fool, the one who justifies what Lear is but not what he has done, the other who condemns what he has done since what he once was he is no longer. Both are right in their respective ways. And Lear is the anomalous subject of the contradiction. If we think only in terms of what he has been accustomed to, we fix too readily upon a man spoiled with power and deference, who finds out now what it is to be an ordinary man. This indeed is the human psychology of his experience, but to see it only in this light is to justify what happens, even to glory in it. The basic attitude of the play contradicts this attitude at every turn.

The feeling Lear has for his fool will bear considerable pondering for the insight it enables us to have. A tender affection in the King leaps across the gulf that separates them, nor is this affection to be explained according to Olivia's famous reminder. Paternal fondness, not forbearance, is what really explains Lear's attitude. He whom many have characterized as constantly demanding flattery recognizes, I believe, an essential loyalty in the barbs of his pure-minded fool, who, in his fashion, takes part with all those in the play whom we call good. The strangeness of the fool persists, however, and continues to elude the simple classification of *good* or *loyal* as we can apply the terms to Gloucester and the disguised Kent (though he does not know the true loyalty in this man who goes by the name of Caius, Lear early expresses gratitude to him and has every reason to regard him as a faithful servant who will follow his master everywhere and under the most trying circumstances). The fool is of no practical help to the King, and his value as a companion is severely limited by the nature of his running commentary. If Lear could simply laugh this off, we would say that he has considerable stoicism, or perhaps indifference—a quality not unlike that which scorns to resent an insult when it comes from those of inferior breed. But the King *is* hurt by the fool. Even when the fool again surprises us by requesting his master to make up with his daughters—

> O Nuncle, Court holy water in a dry house is better than
> this rain water out o' door. Good Nuncle, in, and ask thy
> daughters' blessing. Here's a night pities neither wise man
> nor fool.

— the suggestion, though it would be poison from anyone
else, brings no thundering denunciation from the King. As
Lear sees at last what his evil daughters really are, it may
be that he sees the fool more clearly than we do ourselves:
not a paragon of uncorrupted virtue who prefers honorable
exile to ignominious comfort, but a half-witted boy
severely limited to more practical notions of good and bad.
Whatever he may be, Lear has an affection for him. We
have early evidence of this, much too early for it to be the
last resort of a lonely man whose daughters are all gone
from him. Rather is this affection another side to the
character of Lear, another proof of essential goodness that
was always in him, though it may develop more forcefully
now under the impact of personal affliction.

To those who think otherwise, I can only offer a
general application of the test: Let Authority, of whatever
kind, dispossess itself and endure the full penalty of
banishment. Let it be accompanied by smirking Common
Sense, who derides the mistaken judgment that has led to
this pass. It is a very humane form of authority that can,
under such conditions, turn and say in the words of Lear:

> Poor fool and knave, I have one part in my heart
> That's sorry yet for thee.

In the apparent chaos that whirls about Lear as he goes
forth into the storm, all logic and rationality will seem to
have disappeared. The pairing of the King and the fool
beneath a dazzling bombardment of lightning and thunder

is enough in itself to "turn us all to fools and madmen" as we watch. But all is not as it first appears. We can detect, if we look with sympathy and with faith that outstrips reason, a love between high and low that defies our best-laid plans and our despair alike, and will somehow survive the worst that chaos can do.

The sane and sensible world is, under its conventional appearance, growing rotten in the very emancipation it sought. The ties of duty and the bonds of affection have all been loosened and finally abandoned. Between this world and the storm-swept heath we find it difficult to choose, so evil is the one and so inexplicable the other, but we are likely to feel more at home amid surroundings and rituals that are familiar. A world doomed by reason of its sins, with nothing but chaos all around it—this is the picture which many accept and from which they conclude that the play demonstrates an insane universe devoid of absolutes. They are wrong. Conventions arise from absolutes, not absolutes from conventions, and when the established world dies we are thrown back upon a more primordial form of life, one which seems to bear no similarity to anything we have ever known. Instead of recoiling from it as if it were a horror, we should mark it well, for it is in this maelstrom that we may learn the tremendous consequences of wrong done in the past and what will prove fittest to survive in the future.

VI

THE OUTCAST

The mind of the fool, for all its limitations, sees with uncanny correctness. He says of Regan:

She will taste as like this as a crab does to a crab.

Either an astute observation in the past or something that goes beyond observation must account for this. He has been living with Lear at Albany's palace and has had ample opportunity to see with vision clearer than the King's the demeanor of the household and the growing moods of the mistress who presides. He has not lived with Regan since she has come into her inheritance, but with the intuition of a child, and the certainty of those who are intuitive, he knows what her reception of Lear will be like.

Lear's blindness in failing to see what the fool sees is somewhat misinterpreted, since it is a very special form of blindness that accounts for his persistent faith that he is loved:

Yet have I left a daughter.

Giving the kingdom to Goneril and Regan was, as we have seen, a crime of passion rather than a lapse of judgment. Rage dictated the action, which was punishment for Cordelia rather than reward for her sisters. In the time that has gone by, Lear besides having the opportunity to think more calmly of what he has done, has also seen some of the results. The fool and the knight, the one with biting bluntness and the other with that extreme tactfulness which is a frightening omen, inform him of the "most faint neglect" which he says he has himself noticed:

> which I have rather blamed as mine own jealous curiosity
> than as a very pretense and purpose of unkindness.

In a man whose mind is beginning to weaken because of old age, we would find no difficulty in ascribing to Lear the senile foolishness of one who is already beginning to lose contact with reality. But there is no indication of a wandering intellect, any more than there was at the beginning, and there must be another explanation.

Lear's silence on the subject of Cordelia is not unrelated to his apparent failure to see other unfortunate consequences of the wrong he has done. Persistent wrong-headedness is not due to blindness, necessarily, nor even to arrogance. This caution is particularly apt where love is concerned. If Lear wants to believe that he is loved, in the face of mounting evidence that he is not, let us see him as intensely human before we see him as anything else. One does not turn from a spiteful daughter with the same masculine pride with which he turns from a romantic attachment to a haughty and selfish lady. In the latter case a wounded heart carries honor with it, just as many another wound does. But there is no satisfaction in hating a daughter that once was very dear. She remains a daughter, or, in the words of Lear:

> . . . a disease that's in my flesh
> Which I must needs call mine.

Lear is concerned with the love between himself and his daughters rather than any political results of their rule. What prompted the love test in the first place was love pure and simple. Consequently, his refusal to see the facts before him suggests an enduring need to have his affections requited. With the greatest care Shakespeare subtly indicates this, to the point at which Lear finally sees what he has done his best not to see.

It is a different and a troubled King who greets Regan, trying to express confidence that her feeling for him has not diminished:

> REG. I am glad to see your Highness.
> LEAR. Regan, I think you are, I know what reason
> I have to think so. If thou shouldst not be glad,
> I would divorce me from thy mother's tomb,
> Sepulchring an adultress.

In these words there is more hope than trust.

Regan's answers are a brazen affront to her father's bid for some tokens of affection, but she is motivated only partly, I believe, by her own native unkindness. She is strongly influenced by her older sister, to the point of studiously avoiding any softness that would compromise or in any way reflect upon Goneril's treatment of their father. As a result, her speeches have an unnatural sound, a heightening of tone that makes her manner extremely obvious and impertinent:

> Oh, sir, you are old,
> Nature in you stands on the very verge
> Of her confine. You should be ruled and led
> By some discretion that discerns your state
> Better than you yourself. Therefore I pray you
> That to our sister you do make return.
> Say you have wronged her, sir.

Though an occasional exclamation escapes Lear, he avoids any expression of resentment, preferring to see in her the one loving daughter that will compensate for the loss of the others. Had we no previous knowledge of the talk between Goneril and Regan, or of the message sent in the person of Oswald, or of Kent's account of the way in which this message was received, we would nevertheless understand perfectly the mind of Regan here. Her manner is too pointed to be misread. It is only a question of how long Lear can continue professing her to be that which she is at great pains to demonstrate she is not. His praise of her sounds almost absurd:

> Thy tender-hefted nature shall not give
> Thee o'er to harshness. Her eyes are fierce, but thine
> Do comfort and not burn. 'Tis not in thee
> To grudge my pleasures, to cut off my train,
> To bandy hasty words, to scant my sizes,
> And in conclusion to oppose the bolt
> Against my coming in. Thou better know'st
> The offices of nature, bond of childhood,
> Effects of courtesy, dues of gratitude.
> Thy half o' the kingdom hast thou not forgot,
> Wherein I thee endowed.

Time was when Lear was not slow to react with high indignation to responses far less insulting than Regan's are now. Time was when he questioned her about her love and she replied in the most lavish phrases. Now *he* is making the speech for *her,* and she stands before him unmoved and openly defiant, making only the curt reply:

> Good sir, to the purpose

With Goneril's arrival and the two daughters taking hands in a symbol of their alliance against their father, further pretense on his part becomes futile. The very thing he is attempting to hide must now be revealed in the dramatic situation of Goneril's presence. She has come, obviously, to make certain that Regan does not soften, and

perhaps enable the King to make good his threat to take
back again the reins of government—which he made just
before leaving Albany's palace:

> Thou shalt find
> That I'll resume the shape which thou dost think
> I have cast off forever. Thou shalt, I warrant thee.

With Goneril having come, Lear is moved to demonstrate
to her how different a woman her sister will prove to be:

> I can be patient, I can stay with Regan,
> I and my hundred knights.

But Regan is as eager to show Goneril that she is one with
her as Lear is to show that she is not. Although the
decision has, as we are well aware, already been made the
coming together of all three stresses the conflict between
what the daughters intend and what Lear hopes for. We
anticipate the cold, juridical glance with which Goneril
awaits Regan's reply to her father's confident belief that
he may still have his hundred knights, and the triumphant
satisfaction with which she hears Regan say:

> Not altogether so.
> I looked not for you yet, nor am provided
> For your fit welcome. Give ear, sir, to my sister,
> For those that mingle reason with your passion
> Must be content to think you old, and so—
> But she knows what she does.

It is a devastating blow to Lear's pride, the kind of pride
one takes in those who continue to love him when others
have turned their backs. We can pardon him for wanting to
triumph over Goneril, for wanting to shame her by
contrasting her with a daughter who better knows the
offices of nature. But it is Goneril's triumph, not his. Nor

has he heard the worst.

The proposed reductions in the number of his attendant knights is deliberately calculated to frustrate even his efforts to grasp at the larger number. Goneril has insisted that the knightly escort be reduced from a hundred to fifty. Regan will have it no more than twenty-five. When Lear agrees to the fifty, which "yet doth double five and twenty," Goneril asks what need he has of twenty-five, or ten, or five. "What need one?" asks Regan.

This is the final result of the love test. As Lear stares from one to the other in their stripping of him, he truly feels for the first time what it is to be a "poor old man, as full of grief as age, wretched in both." But it is a commanding figure we see reduced to this, and therein lies the pathos. Lear is no Pere Goriot, despite the parallel of an aged father abandoned by two selfish daughters. We see a monarch who yet bears in his countenance the authority that Kent reverences, and it is this that touches us most in the man who is deprived of everything and bursts from his daughters' presence with the terrible cry:

"O fool, I shall go mad!"

Out of the gorgeous palace goes Lear, away from all the royal splendor, the comforts and finery of life, and onto a deluged and barren heath where life is exposed to the fury of the elements. We can do worse than forget for the moment the distinctions signified in all the regalia of the former life and dwell realistically upon the physical discomfort of those who have known better days. But it is better to recall it and all that it means. War as it was fought in those days had a glory and a splendor to it, for all the hardship it entailed, and forces us to dwell upon the contrasting plainness of Lear's sufferings, stripped as he is of every banner, actual and symbolic. The King, the nobleman, the gentleman, the fool make their unsteady way through showers of rain, the whole lit up for a brief second like midday and then plunged into blackness amid explosions of thunder. The very earth shakes like a thing unfirm under the pounding:

> The wrathful skies
> Gallow the very wanderers of the dark
> And make them keep their caves. Since I was man,
> Such sheets of fire, such bursts of horrid thunder,
> Such groans of roaring wind and rain, I never
> Remember to have heard. Man's nature cannot carry
> The affliction nor the fear.

These words of honest Kent remind us that, while the tempest within Lear is the major one, this other is fierce and has its symbolic meaning. There is no destination. Whither do their wanderings lead them?

If we have in our minds a true perception of the King, drawn from the most careful consideration of everything that has happened so far, we are one with Lear and feel within ourselves the force of his insanity as the storm bursts again and again over his head. It is a powerful and aggressive Lear who goes insane. Strength, not weakness, characterizes his madness every step of the way, and age is no more than a contributing factor—more indirect than direct. No one can even begin to do justice to these marvelous storm scenes. But if we are ready for them as the play has prepared us to be, their effect will measure up to the power that is in them. When I say "prepared us," I do not mean that we expect them. Quite the reverse. They tear assunder this image of royal authority, unbalance it, drive it to madness. The downfall is dramatic in the extreme and worthy of the poetry in which it is expressed. It is not a sad story that Shakespeare is telling us, but a disaster.

Over the years Lear has, as we have seen, held a power

that through constant use has developed the strength of his personality, just as surely as continual physical activity will develop the body. His wise and proper use of that power I have already given my reasons for believing. Whole volumes might be written in defense of or in dispute of the merits of kingship, but, while the subject is not without some bearing, it need not prejudice us one way or the other, and I must leave it at that. What I am more concerned with here is the strength this power imparts to the one who has long possessed it—an idea we seem never to understand except as it applies to a tyrant, so enamored have we become of the famous dictum that absolute power corrupts absolutely. That it often does cannot be denied, and I share as much as anyone the fear of one person possessing too much of it. I deny, however, that *King Lear* is a study of such a case.

The play is not political nor is it concerned with forms of government. Lear is the head of a kingdom, or has been till he divested himself of the cares of state. But he symbolizes something more than political rule. Kent's famous reference to him as king, father, master and patron expresses a veneration almost religious in character (the passage in which he says this is itself a disclaimer of all obsequiousness), as if Lear represented the true ideal he had always followed. Lear is indeed emblematic, and as we listen to these words of Kent, we see their justification fully evidenced in the living presence, the form, the lineament and feature of the King. The difficulty of picturing Lear thus is not due to any lack of imagination, but to the bias of recent centuries against reverence in any form. Man cannot bestow reverence upon what he does not in all honesty accept. This is simply to say that it should be neither pretended nor misplaced. But irreverence for its own sake is nothing but the starvation of a deeply religious appetite, which will bite into dangerous weeds if it cannot have its proper food, and in the play we have several notable examples of what may well be the logical result: obsequiousness without reverence.

To say that we no longer accept royalty and must therefore reject the hypotheses of *King Lear* [22] is to remove the play from its rank as high tragedy and put it on an absurdly lower plain: a relic from a bygone age or a treatise on annointed majesty, taking the opposite position from Milton's *Tenure of Kings and Magistrates.*

Many have seen Lear as a microcosm, which I believe to be essentially true and only saying in a general way what can be said more specifically. In representing the people he rules, he is an ideal of society, not a perfect type but rather a symbol of social order. What happens to Lear happens to the world he represents. If we combine evidence with likelihood, we discern the only kind of character suited to the poetry he speaks: not a dying institution, but a vigorous one with an amazing power to endure the worst, and whose threatened destruction makes us reflect more deeply what he has signified in the past and what his death might bode for the future. Does Lear's great age mean no more than that he is old and feeble? Must we insist as Regan does, or affects to do?

> I pray you, Father, being weak, seem so.

The answer is that, though Lear is old, he is not weak. Well may we wonder whether Shakespeare did not detect in the story a meaning beyond that of rugged strength, whether in fact a man who endures so much in the extremities of age does not suggest a durability beyond that of less worthy lives. The play gives us reason for thinking so. Those enemies of the King: Goneril, Regan, Cornwall, Edmund, Oswald—Lear survives them all. When he dies at the end, those who believed in him are the ones who remain alive. Some kind of permanence lies beneath these facts.

Consequently, the figure of an outcast Lear is one of strength in paralysis. The madness that ensues is a whirlwind of passion, raving and incoherent in its reaction to the incongruous situation and struggling fiercely in its helplessness, rather than the simple decay of a super-annuated intellect. Lear's insanity is indeed Miltonic, as Lamb saw very clearly. In the grandeur of madness we read the grandeur of what Lear once was, much more than we read it in the loyalty of Kent, though it must be confessed that Kent confirms what is manifest in the anguish of these highly poetic scenes. We once gazed upon him as he refused to hear mention of Cordelia, and we wondered at the sorrow within—over which he was king. Now he is king over nothing, not even himself, as all the force that once expended itself in rule bursts incoherently forth, like machinery that ruptures because it can no longer function properly. This is the madness of Lear: the madness of forceful power. Like the blood of Duncan, who would have thought the old man could have so much in him? The workings of the mind, like the organs of the body, are hideous when they gush out into view. A powerful intellect, like the bursting machine it resembles, displays its strength more when it snaps apart than when it worked so smoothly we regarded it not.[23]

We never forget that Lear *is* a king, yet in his outcast state he transcends, it seems to me, the limited concept of political ruler and takes on the image of something much more. Not in the royal court only, but in degrading circumstances that are greater tests of the love he inspires we see him followed with unflagging devotion. "Leave all and follow me." Kent and the fool—the high and the low—are there, and Gloucester comes to the aid of the King, "Though I die for it, as no less is threatened me." If I had to choose from the pages of literature a royal figure that best exemplifies that which is to be honored, I can think of none better than Lear. His sin, regrettable as it is, makes him more human, more actual, just as a perfect Lear would only be artificial for all that he would theoretically deserve more esteem than the sinful Lear does.

Amid all the boiling disaster, we are aware of a purpose which the forces of evil have violated. Once having seen that purpose as Lear himself, a purpose that must be a mighty one if it is to have any meaning at all, we are roused by the fearfulness of his being pounded by the elements and driven to insanity. The dignity and royal bearing are gone, but the strength which sustained them reveals itself in the most intense passion:

> Contending with the fretful elements.
> Bids the wind blow the earth into the sea,
> Or swell the curlèd waters 'bove the main,
> That things might change or cease; tears his white hair,
> Which the impetuous blasts, with eyeless rage,
> Catch in their fury, and make nothing of;
> Strives in his little world of man to outscorn
> The to-and-fro-conflicting wind and rain.

The pity we have for Lear as a man is almost drowned in a more powerful kind of pity, that which we feel for the sovereign refusing to weaken even in a state of utter helplessness. Not all the sentimentality of Richard II can move us as the raging fury of Lear does.

The "superstitious" belief to which the Elizabethans seemingly held, that "the heavens themselves blaze forth the death of princes," is more defensible than the unsuperstitious naturalism of today. Like Edmund, we reject the astrological relationship and replace it with nothing. The most confirmed cynic on these matters, if he has any insight into the poetry of Shakespeare, would not regard the storm as a purely accidental occurrence, and thereby leave us to wonder how the story might have gone had Lear been driven out on a beautiful moonlit night in the middle of June. On the other hand the most ardent believer is not likely to say that the treatment of Lear has *caused* the storm, or that the storm is some kind of preternatural manifestation at the fall of a king. Yet there is a relationship, one we accept without seeking any further explanation than that the storm comes almost at the precise moment Lear leaves Gloucester's castle, and expends all its fury as he wanders about on the heath. If the more naturalistic among us demand satisfaction, the answer can always be made that storms would come sooner or later, winter would certainly come, and the dispossessed King would experience the full extent of "houseless poverty." That he experiences it now may be but literary convenience. When we have discussed the question to everyone's satisfaction, however, I believe we are left with a large measure of the inexplicable, the force of which was there to begin with, and it is made neither more nor less acceptable by fetching after probability.

Lear the outcast and the stormy chaos of the heavens are in a symbolic relationship. We approve absolutely the license of the poet in weaving a background for the eviction of Lear as the royal surroundings were for his initial appearance as ruling monarch. We might as well analyze the robes of the reigning Lear as ask why there is a storm when he is cast forth. Meaning is all, and it must be apprehended. Probability—that which is likely to occur—is but the imitation of life's shallow exterior, more disguise than reality.

Lear is the chief victim of this tempest that accompanies his downfall. Thus, the sign or symbol directs its fury at him, as if its meaning were intended, not as a rebuke to those who have despoiled the King of his proper status, but as a rebuke to the King himself. "What is the cause of thunder?" he asks after his wits have begun to turn. Later he remarks that the thunder would not cease at his bidding. The mystery of thunder and its indifference

even to the commands of a king are as meaningful as its
reflecting in the heavens the chaos that exists upon earth.
Its punitive force, its unknown origin, its power, its
tenacity of purpose suggest in an occult way something
transcendental—one is almost tempted to think of it as the
wrath of superior powers at the crucifixion of their
designee on earth, except that we know Lear to be a sinner
and that it is his sin that is in a large way responsible for all
this. He is the cause of his own crucifixion rather than the
innocent victim of the sins of others.

It is this concept of the sinful King enduring the results
of his sin that I believe fixes upon Lear the royalty we
have so many other means of seeing. The very heavens
afflict him. The sin of which he has been guilty, the
violation of true love, becomes a sin of cosmic proportions
because of him who committed it! Not a man merely, but
a ruler of men, a voice of the highest authority, a true
representative of the gods on earth has violated the only
thing whereby authority, rule and order are possible. His
greatness has alone made his sin great, though such a sin is
not small even among the humblest. Most will be asked
from those to whom most is given. A variation of this
Scriptural admonition is almost self-evident: he who holds
the greatest authority has power to do the greatest good or
the greatest evil. No official act of his is unimportant. The
very impunity his power would seem to give him is the
most misleading thing about the position he occupies.
Instead of assuring him, it ought always to caution him.

Consequently, the stripping away of everything from
Lear is, indeed, a form of condign punishment, but not in
the sense that many have understood it. The irony of a
king learning what it is to be an ordinary mortal is quite
visible but hardly the central purpose of Lear's outcast
state. What he must learn, or rather *learn once again,* is
what true authority is and all the things upon which it
rests—the chief of which is love. He does become purified,

in the purgatorial sense, as he also becomes enlightened, but the particular kind of purification and enlightenment concern the exercise of authority in its relationship to love. If Hamlet were sinless he would be the perfect man. If Lear were sinless he would be the perfect king.

Failure to see this makes of *King Lear* the story of a man—which it is, but much more—and reduces all significance to trivia. The result is that the horrendous storm effects and the deaths of so many characters are "out of all proportion," as indeed they would be in such a reduced interpretation, and we are left with the "loosely-knit play."

In the philosophical epilogue of Tolstoy's novel *War and Peace,* the author denies that power can be explained in terms of the powerful man only, since the vastness of military and political operations cannot conceivably grow out of some unique talent of the man himself. Circumstances, voluntary cooperation on the part of followers, and many other considerations all play their part, and not until we discover a cause equal to the effect, says Tolstoy, can we explain something as vast as the Napoleonic invasion of Russia. Whether or not one happens to agree with Tolstoy, we are left with the problem of explaining political power, in peace as well as in war, and whether the dividing of power lessens it in the aggregate. The little man who is fortunate enough to possess his share in a democratic society knows not, oftentimes, that he is a little Lear wielding the same kind of authority, and, though he has considerably less of it, he may make the same mistake Lear did, in exercising what he considers to be his to do with as he chooses. An entire nation of Lears might possibly bring about a result not unlike that of the play we are discussing—with perhaps something of the mystery as to how so much can come of so little. It is *not* little! The cause is equal to the effect.

In stressing the enormity of Lear's guilt, I wish at the

same time to insist on the point I have been making all along: that Lear is guilty in no other way. He has been a good king:

A father, and a gracious agèd man
Whose reverence even the head-lugged bear would lick . . .

But to see this particular guilt as trivial poses the necessity of adding other sins to make up the difference. There is no need to refute all over again this interpretation of Lear, but I must point out the psychological truth that lies concealed beneath it. The collapse of what is truly good is more awful to contemplate than the collapse of evil. Freeing a nation from the rule of a wicked or ineffectual king may have its dire consequences, as Shakespeare's history plays demonstrate, but we have to search long and hard for a case parallel to Lear's: that of a good and able king deposed. His story is the stranger in that no foreign invader or rival claimant to the throne has deposed him; he has done it to himself and has put others in charge—the kind of rulers they turn out to be we already know. The kind of ruler Lear has been makes all the difference. I say that if we accept all evidence and reasonable interpretation, and conceive of a goodly king, a capable and impressive ruler for whom the people of Britain had an abiding reverence, we share the psychology of those loyal ones who have watched the most honored supremacy do wrong and stumble into an ignominious descent. A bad king or a senile one could never inspire the sense of tragedy Lear does. Only if we know him for what he truly is can we give vent to the ejaculation:

O thou side-piercing sight!

VII

THE PENITENT

In the reaction of Lear to the storm many see a kind of confession of the wrongs they insist have characterized his reign as king. The selfish monarch, they feel, is established beyond question by such damning evidence as is apparently contained in the following oft-quoted passage:

Poor naked wretches, wheresoe'er you are,
That bide the pelting of this pitiless storm,
How shall your houseless heads and unfed sides,
Your looped and windowed raggedness, defend you
From seasons such as these? Oh, I have ta'en
Too little care of this! Take physic, pomp.
Expose thyself to feel what wretches feel,
That thou mayst shake the superflux to them
And show the Heavens more just.

Attempts are sometimes made to corroborate that all-important line "I have ta'en too little care of this!" with other quotations that indicate the kind of justice being practiced by those in office:

A man may see how this world goes with no eyes. Look with thine ears. See how yond Justice rails upon yond simple thief. Hark, in thine ear. Change places and, handy-dandy, which is the Justice, which is the thief?

And a few lines further:

A dog's obeyed in office.
Thou rascal beadle, hold thy bloody hand!
Why dost thou lash that whore? Strip thine own back.
Thou hotly lust'st to use her in that kind
For which thou whip'st her. The usurer hangs the cozener.
Through tattered clothes small vices do appear,
Robes and furred gowns hide all. Plate sin with gold
And the strong lance of justice hurtless breaks.

What we are given apparently, is a picture of corrupt institutions, for which Lear as king must bear a large part of the blame. Has he been blind? The theme of blindness, both figurative and actual, provides a rich store of such apt quotes as "See better, Lear," and leaves us with the imputation of criminal negligence or ineptness, neither of which is easy to forgive in a king. Has he permitted venality? This is difficult to believe. However, we must answer the question one way or the other if Lear's "admissions" are to be taken in anything like the sense in which many read them.

First of all, I would agree that the argument of insanity carries little weight. What the King says, though it lacks form a little, is not like madness. We know him to vary between sanity and insanity in these later scenes, "matter and impertinency mixed," but the thoughts he expresses here are something more than incoherent ravings. We must, however, allow for the experience of one who learns that there is no art to find the mind's construction in the face. Lear has been betrayed by those on whom he has built an absolute trust. The facts of which he speaks have the ring of truth, but truths generalized by bitter cynicism. One sad betrayal makes all mankind hypocrite. It is this same cynical spirit that prompts Lear to extend forgiveness for adultery:

I pardon that man's life. What was thy cause? Adultery?
Thou shalt not die. Die for adultery! No.

The wren goes to 't, and the small gilded fly
Does lecher in my sight.
Let copulation thrive, for Gloucester's bastard son
Was kinder to his father than my daughters
Got 'tween the lawful sheets.

None shall be punished where sin proves itself better than virtue.

Undoubtedly there have been men of simular virtue whose robes and furred gowns hid all, while small vices appeared through tattered clothes. How much Lear was aware of this before is a moot point, but it is not likely that he knows more now than he knew when he was king. Cynicism partly explains the impulse to condemn all and to punish none, as evidenced by his belief that Gloucester's bastard son was kinder than his own daughters. But there is something else.

If Lear had been gradually weakening, both mentally and physically, prior to the time of his actual insanity, it does not seem at all likely that he would attain this recovery—and a vigorous one it is—after all he has been through. Tracing his insanity from very early in the play, as many are wont to do, leads to the strange paradox of this aggressive, active language spoken in the sunlight and beautiful weather, unlike the darker incoherence of the night and storm. The light here is as symbolic as was the darkness. Lear reasserts his kingship: "Aye, every inch a king," with discordant snatches of the old authority that issued directives and was obeyed. The king rather than the father, or even the man, assumes a status that has been lost and peremptorily gives commands to figures who are not there. This is the Lear that we recall from the first scene:

When I do stare, see how the subject quakes.

The authoritative note in his voice is balanced, however,

with an admission of delusion on his part and what appears to be a cynical conviction of the wrongdoing of those in office and those who are subject to them. Lear, every inch a king, nevertheless shares the general weakness and imperfection of those beneath him:

> They flattered me like a dog, and told me I had white hairs in my beard ere the black ones were there. To say "aye" and "no" to everything that I said! "Aye" and "no" too was no good divinity. When the rain came to wet me once and the wind to make me chatter, when the thunder would not peace at my bidding, there I found 'em, there I smelt 'em out. Go to, they are not men o' their words. They told me I was everything. 'Tis a lie, I am not ague-proof.

The apparent conflict might be explained as the beginning of wisdom wherein facts when first seen tend to confuse rather than clarify. To Lear the old power to command must in some way still seem right and proper. Yet it was shot through with lies. He was told he was wise, and he was flattered with continual acquiescence to whatever he said. He was assured that he was everything. It is a lie. Still, he is king, and though he pardons that man's adultery he cannot forbear remarking how the subject quakes at his royal glance.

Old habits and new discoveries appear to be in opposition. There is considerable truth to this, though I would distinguish between "realization through experience"—for which there is no substitute—and knowledge that is completely new. Lear never believed that he was literally proof against the ague, any more than he believed that he was "everything." Undoubtedly the flattery that kings are always heir to succeeded in dimming the meaningfulness of his own limitations, and a storm-swept heath brought it home to him again. We can understand this much without reasoning to a Lear utterly blind to his own humanity and consequently ruling as if he had the power of divinity to say "aye" and "no" to everything.

Far from a pointless clue to an equally pointless authoritarianism, Lear's speeches have here a deeper meaning that is concerned with the central theme of the plot. When he speaks in this contradictory fashion, he is in flight from Cordelia:

> A sovereign shame so elbows him. His own unkindness
> That stripped her from his benediction, turned her
> To foreign casualties, gave her dear rights
> To his doghearted daughters. These things sting
> His mind so venomously that burning shame
> Detains him from Cordelia.

More than her apparent bluntness in the love test would the very sight of her now be a reproach to him. How much does this "sovereign shame" at his own sin affect his attitude toward the sins of others? Misanthropy is the usual alternative to the embarrassments of sentiment. Proclaiming the evils of mankind becomes a triumphant kind of wisdom, more expressive in its way than yielding to the softness of persevering love, and Lear is human enough in this regard. But his is a more powerful reason than that of most in preferring the discovery of evil to the discovery of goodness, since the one enables him to denounce in kingly fashion the sins of the world, from which he has himself suffered dreadfully, whereas the other forces him to dwell on his own terrible mistake and the forgiveness that yet awaits him.

When Lear awakens in Cordelia's presence he is a very different person. The insanity seems to have left him completely and he becomes in his own words, a "foolish fond old man." He is humble and contrite before the searing effect of her forgiveness:

> If you have poison for me, I will drink it.
> I know you do not love me, for your sisters
> Have, as I do remember, done me wrong.
> You have some cause, they have not.

Though this speech comes from his heart, it is not easy for him to say it and it was a great deal more difficult to contemplate saying it. When he shunned Cordelia in his mad resumption of kingship, Lear preferred to think of the evil to be found in women:

> Down from the waist they are Centaurs,
> Though women all above.
> But to the girdle do the gods inherit,
> Beneath is all the fiends'.

As goodness shames him Lear plunges back to the memory of his wicked daughters rather than dwell on the virtue that will remind him of Cordelia. In a previous scene the ingratitude of Goneril and Regan upset him even to think upon: "Oh, that way madness lies." But madness this time is a comfort rather than a scourge, just as pretended kingship is a refuge from the foolish old man he must acknowledge himself to be if he is to face the truth. It is here rather than when he tears at his clothes with "Off, off, you lendings!" that Lear comes to this realization. Instead of tearing off anything, he crowns himself:

> ... with rank fumiter and furrow weeds,
> With burdocks, hemlock, nettles, cuckoo flowers,
> Darnel, and all the idle weeds that grow
> In our sustaining corn.

Here indeed is matter and impertinency mixed. He would once again be the thing he was.

How little all this matters to Cordelia, how far from her thoughts is any sense of triumph or readiness to take advantage of the situation, is apparent from the way she addresses him. "How does my royal lord?" she calls out softly as he awakens, and "How fares your Majesty?" This, following the most tender sentiments which she expresses while he is still asleep, is an insistence upon the honor he still deserves. The helpless old father and the King are one and the same with her. Henceforth simplicity never leaves him. Cordelia does indeed triumph, not in the vindictive manner a lesser person would have been tempted to do, but in the very way Lear may have feared. His willingness to drink poison is the last vestige of resistance: punishment seems more palatable than forgiveness. But her "No cause, no cause" is more than a gentle denial to ease her father's guilty feelings. Cordelia's devotion remains constant, unlike her sisters' "love" that found in every petty annoyance a "cause," and she can deny with absolute truth that her father's sin has ever given her any reason to cease loving him.

In this utter simplicity of a weak old man Lear is finally brought face to face with what he once banished. Perhaps it is only in such a state that he can be made to realize what he has lost and found again. Does Shakespeare thereby suggest that there is such a disparity between authority and love, much as one depends on the other, that the one must be lost before the other can come to know it? It is not necessarily true that what happens in Shakespeare is to be set down as a rigid principle from which we dare not make exception, but I would venture to say that the two tend to move away from each other and the more authoritarian and the more loving each one is respectively, the less they can work together. Of the two, love alone is self-sufficient. Authority by itself is self-destructive. Lear has been a good king and a loving father, but his great error came when he appointed himself as judge of who loved him most and permitted his kingly character to make the decision. He need not have decided as he did—kings may see rightly, nor is the kingly vocation the only one to make a man forgetful—but once having made that fateful mistake he is destined to find the truth only after he is stripped of all authority and lies helpless in the arms of love.

He made his desperate attempt to flee, not because he was ever inimical to love, but because he came to feel the burden of having inflicted a wound upon it. He would be king again, the only identity he can seek beyond love's pale. Bizarre attempts to command and to forgive become a kind of hysteria with him, and even this is interrupted by those who pursue in love's name. Again he flees. But fear wist not to evade as love wist to pursue.

The beauty of Lear's reconciliation with Cordelia is shown both in what he has had to surrender in order to come by it and what she has had to keep in order to seek it. To call the reconciliation unashamedly sentimental is to take Lear's way of shunning the beauty of it, without even the excuse that he had. Shakespeare knew how to treat such things, uncomfortable as we may feel with other authors who make the same attempt. The romantic comedies are proof enough that Shakespeare, without in any way undervaluing the true emotions of love, had as little patience as anyone could with the silly artificialities to which lovers are sometimes prone. In *King Lear* love is the very heart of a tremendous story, and it is unpardonable to take these scenes between Cordelia and her father as any less poetic than scenes of greater energy or supposedly deeper intellectual value.[24]

It has become almost hackneyed to repeat anything so well known as the Elizabethan concept of hierarchy, according to which the body politic depended upon the throne. It is of paramount importance to any consideration of monarchy in Shakespeare. Yet in this, the most monarchical of his plays, this element has not been sufficiently appreciated, and in many cases it is entirely misread. If *Lear* were a political play, we would be as much aware of hierarchical order as we are in the history plays. But such political action as we find — the division between the dukes, the French invasion—are given only cursory treatment and are important only as they relate to what is nonpolitical. This is, however, a tragedy of monarchy, unlike so many Elizabethan plays that portray the downfall of kings and are really tragedies of ambition, pride, lust, misrule and various other sins or tragic defects that deface monarchy rather than exemplify it. The search for the tragic defect in Lear invariably leads to *pride* or *misrule* or to some psychological analysis of his *dotage,* none of which holds up under scrutiny, and instead of giving us fresh insights into the tragedy, succeeds only in confusing it. Yet it remains a tragedy of monarchy, going right to the heart of the subject and probing it in all its human psychology.

It is this human psychology that so engulfs many that they neglect the real subject and view the play as the story of an old man (variously interpreted) with three daughters—meanwhile taking a hostile view of the kingly status of Lear, as if his royal authority were not only bad but quite unnecessary and his long reign a form of presumptuousness on his part. The only sympathy they can engender for him relates to the pathetic old man cruelly abused by ungrateful daughters.

The actual Lear is the one at whose stare the subject would quake. Now he is an old man in truth, lying in bed, spent and tired. Are all thy glories come to this? We do not ask the question in the same spirit as Mark Antony asks it of the corpse of Caesar, but we do experience a disbelief that is almost as great. No tragic ending here, but life's simplicities stripping the King of all ornamentation as thoroughly as tragedy could do, yet bestowing love and respect nonetheless. No more need be said. Such scenes lose more than they gain by analysis or comment. If, as is so often true of Shakespeare's dramatic structure, we have seen action and character in the proper light, we are ready for the simplicity of his homelier little incidents. Taken by themselves they are not essentially different from those of lesser authors. But coming as fulfillment of the most careful preparation, they achieve an effect impossible in stories that are not nearly as vivid. What is actually spoken between father and daughter as they become reunited we could easily improvise ourselves and be very close to Shakespeare. It is enough for us to realize that the father is Lear and the daughter is Cordelia, whom no one but Shakespeare could have created. If they are strangers to us, if indeed we have misconstrued their characters (Cordelia is proud and reserved, Lear is arrogance drooping into dotage), we are in the position of one who is informed that the person to whom he has been speaking has just been through a harrowing experience and is now being talked about throughout the world. If only we had known in time! How much more closely we would have looked and listened, even though we did listen and heard every word distinctly. Better to know afterwards than never to know at all.

A Shakespearean passage always loses something when taken out of context, but none loses so much as the one with that unaffected simplicity which is so much a part of life. As Lear's greatness makes great the wrongs he commits, so it lends greatness to this conclusion wherein his wrongs are expiated and the daughter he banished "forever" has come back to him. We tend momentarily to forget that Cordelia is actually the Queen of France, and to think of her as a loving daughter only, but Lear has commanded center stage throughout and the magic of Shakespeare's poetry has made the man and the king so vivid that we are compelled to see amid this little episode of reunion and recovery a dynasty coming to a close.

All this is obscured if we take the King's earlier

"admissions" in another and quite disconnected sense from the one intended. His references to the lives of the miserable poor and the "too little care" he has taken of them, his ejaculation to "take physic, pomp," and shake the superflux to those in dire need, hardly seem like a confession of callous indifference in his own past. Is it possible that any but the most ideally perfect king who ever lived can realize the true meaning of chill penury? I do not deny that in being reduced to the status of a beggar Lear is seeing life in a way he never saw it before. What impresses me is the sympathy he shows for all who must live as he is living now. A Lear guided exclusively by selfishness and pride would be wholly taken up by his own sad lot, and if he thought at all about others it would be an afterthought when the fury of the tempest had long ceased.

Henry IV in his soliloquy on sleep and Henry V in his long meditation on what "infinite heartsease must kings neglect that private men enjoy," both give a very different picture of what it is like to be poor. Feeling the intense pressure of responsibility, a king may be pardoned for envying those who lie in smoky cribs upon uneasy pallets or get them to bed crammed with distressful bread, though such envy is the dream of the castle: a negative idealization of what the simple life is free from rather than what it is bound by. It may be that in Lear's younger days he had similar ideas. We do not know. If he had, he may have been lulled by his own fancies into believing that life among the lowly is a beautiful thing, and then thought no more about it. It is only a guess, but it would fit the character who personifies royalty in its weaknesses as well as its strengths.

In admitting that he has taken too little care, not only do we not know what he means by "too little"—how little is *too little*?—but he demonstrates an honesty about himself, a contrite heart and at least some purpose of amendment. Envy, if Lear was guilty of it in common with other kings, is invariably a form of blindness which permits us to see only the good side of what someone else possesses, be it ever so little, but obscures the bad. Let us condemn him for nothing worse than what the play shows him to be: human like the rest of us. When we have admitted that, we have said the worst. But we have not destroyed that other Lear who has merited the love of those whom the play teaches us to admire.

There is something symbolic in Edgar's tricking of Gloucester into taking a little fall instead of a great one. The similarity between the two plots suggests many points of comparison and contrast, and Gloucester, who is dispossessed of land and castle and, after being blinded, is thrust out of doors to "smell his way to Dover," suffers worse affliction than Lear does. The fall, however, is a lesser one by comparison. Each father learns a philosophy of resignation as a result and is the better led by the faithful son and the faithful daughter. Taken by itself, Lear's fall into the loving care of Cordelia is as little a thing as Gloucester's pitching forward on level ground. In the mind of each it is immense, the one eager for it and the other trying to avoid it, though both seek to escape what they are unable to face.

From little things do great things come. Simplicity by itself has little meaning. Only a great mind can see its vastness. Next to the great mind is that mind that has known greatness and finds itself forced back to life's very elementals, yet has eyes to see into them. If this be true it will be true unto death, and any resumption of the former life will be a paltry thing indeed. Lear is brought low, but he undergoes a progress too enormous to be measured by the things of this world. The lightning-like glitter of eternity shakes through the little sentiments of this mighty King who goes not to a royal death but to a miserable end.

Yet prior to this he is thoroughly converted to what he fled from before. Those versions of the Lear story according to which he becomes king again seem so natural that we can detect an artifice whereby Shakespeare has his protagonist make the same attempt and fail because quite another fate lies in store for him. The dictates of nature are strong, but the result is incoherent. Something we hesitate to call the supernatural—partly from native disbelief, partly from a lack of what we conventionally imagine the voices of the gods to be like—beckons another way. Lear is drawn there in spite of himself and speaks words he never spoke as King:

> We two alone will sing like birds i' the cage.
> When thou dost ask me blessing, I'll kneel down
> And ask of thee forgiveness. So we'll live,
> And pray, and sing, and tell old tales, and laugh
> At gilded butterflies . . .

These words have the simple enthusiasm we associate with children. Yet there is something almost terrible about them. They are *childlike* without being *childish,* and Lear is childlike without being in his second childhood. The desire to live a life in which love colors the plainest things with poetic beauty is impregnated with a thought just as simple but with a strange echo of mysticism:

> And take upon 's the mystery of things
> As if we were God's spies.

This *is* the new Lear, one we cannot explain in terms of what he was in the past, or according to some scientific process whereby his wits are once again beginning to turn. He speaks, moreover, under the cloud of defeat; the battle is lost and our fears (soon to be confirmed) as to what Edmund means to do surround father and daughter with an ominous atmosphere.

Something strikes us here, so very different from the nature of impending tragedy as to sound strangely discordant. Sweet simplicity when heard amid tones more sombre is weird and dissonant. In the transformed King as well as in the circumstances in which we find him we hear the eerie voice of a child.

VIII

THE DEATH OF CORDELIA

The sufferings of Lear, the truths he undergoes such agony to learn, his final descent—or is it a rise?—into a peaceful simplicity constitute a purification that may be thought of as purgatorial. In our own limited concept and in a looser understanding of the word, we may think of it as a way of redeeming one who is guilty of evil but not by specific design. Weakness, blindness, temptation, the passion of the moment—all these, even to a limited degree, not only lessen the guilt but mark it as an essentially different kind of evil from that which is consciously intended and carefully plotted.

From a purely secular point of view, the question must be left unresolved as to whether Lear has expiated his sin in a religious sense and therefore deserves the happiness of another world. We do not know what happens to him after death. The reward which the secular mind insists upon, not illogically, since it would rule out heaven as beyond the limits of the play, is the happy ending: Lear peacefully reunited with Cordelia, all his loyal followers rejuvenated and preparing to live "happily ever after." Since this does not happen, the intense suffering which Lear undergoes would seem to lead nowhere but to a tragic and unfulfilling downfall. An eternity of bliss after death is a mere presumption; granted that we can neither affirm nor deny it, we cannot offer a *possibility* as the ultimate end toward which Shakespeare's powerful tragedy leads. The stark reality of what we see blots out visions and theories

as to what happens next, since every theatre-goer is
entitled to his own opinion anyway.

This entire question, a much debated one, has considerable bearing on my own particular subject, since what
the character of Lear has represented in life cannot be
separated from its meaning in death. The way in which he
ruled determines the one; the manner in which he dies
determines the other. Taken alone, the fact of death is not
in itself tragic, at least not nearly so as the death of
Othello, of Desdemona, Hamlet, Romeo, Juliet, and many
others, all of whom are considerably younger than Lear
and had much to live for had they not been brought to an
untimely end. Lear is a very old man:

> The wonder is he hath endured so long.
> He but usurped his life.

Lear's death, however, is not one that comes simply as a
result of having lived out the allotted span of life—longer
in his case—as is true, say, of Henry IV. The *Henry IV*
duology ends with the death of Henry, perhaps hastened
by vexations not unlike those of Lear, yet we do not
classify as tragedy a work in which the protagonist (the
titular protagonist, if not the actual one) dies peacefully,
reconciled to his errant son, and triumphant over his
enemies. Lear is consumed with anguish, at least till the
very moment of death, about which scholars are in
disagreeement: does he die in ecstasy as Bradley thought,[25]
or in despair, as Elton insists?[26]

We can perhaps all agree that death is at least some
kind of blessed release from the sufferings Lear has
endured. As Kent says of him:

> Vex not his ghost. Oh, let him pass! He hates him
> That would upon the rack of this tough world
> Stretch him out longer.

But the events immediately prior to his death, and possibly the actual cause of it, whether or not he might have lived much longer, form the real tragedy. Lear has been reunited with Cordelia and in a way "saved," both in the literal sense of being given refuge after long being an outcast, and in the somewhat more spiritual sense of finding peace of soul. But the forces of Cordelia are defeated in battle and Edmund treacherously orders the death of the King and Cordelia. Though Edmund later rescinds the order, it is too late. Cordelia is hanged and Lear comes on stage carrying her dead body.[27]

Cordelia's death, tragic in every sense of the word, has occasioned considerable comment. It has been called a senseless piece of cruelty and its effect on Lear a devastating blow, coming as it does just when the cycle of action is thought to be complete. A gratuitous act of horror is thrown in at the point at which the story might have come to a happier ending. Classical tragedy, which grows more and more ominous, in a way prepares us for a fate that seems almost inescapable, and we accept the most dreadful outcome as if it were preordained. Shakespeare, on the other hand, seems to have prepared us for a happy consummation of Lear's progress toward love, only to confront us with the bitterest of disappointments. Blasted of every hope he had, Lear goes into a death-agony from which he cannot recover. Regardless of what the play or character might mean to this point, the ending would seem to crown all. The long, tortuous path leads but to this. Is the world of Lear an insane one, and if it is, can Lear himself have any meaning in it?

First of all, the death of Cordelia cannot be defended on any such ground as that it ought to happen or that it accords with some code of justice. Neither can the death of Antigonus or the murder of Duncan. This one may be more terrible than other tragic deaths in Shakespeare, but that does not make the others right or in any way suggestive of an ordered universe, which the hanging of Cordelia would seem to disprove. The crime is a terrible one, the more so for the precise moment at which it occurs. But those who reason to an insane universe on the strength of it are making assumptions which they do not really understand, and which in any event must be applied to all tragedies wherein the innocent are put to death, or for that matter to every case in which injustice is practiced. Because injustice exists, goes the assumption, there is no such thing as justice, as if the two were mutually and entirely exclusive and could not possibly occur at the same time and place. We might just as well say that the tricking of Sir Andrew Aguecheek into a duel with Viola proves that the world of *Twelfth Night* is a rambling chaos in which there are no absolute values. Sir Andrew may be a simpleton, but how do we define the term if we are to use it as sanction for frightening someone half to death with tales of the terrible "firago" who means to have at him? Simpletons have rights like everyone else, particularly if they are innocent of any wrongdoing, and if poor Sir Andrew were to be hanged in a cell I doubt that we would react as we do to the hanging of Cordelia. What he does suffer is the fear that he *may* be put to death, which none of us would care to undergo, but we can enjoy it in one who is simply "matter for a May morning."

The horror that many feel over the execution of Cordelia establishes the very thing it is supposed to contradict: an innate sense of justice and a powerful indignation when justice is violated. For us Cordelia represents love and innocence as few characters in Shakespeare are able to. Killing her is like killing goodness itself. But if killing goodness implies that goodness never existed in the first place—a metaphysical contradiction right there!—then Cordelia's death has no significance whatever, nor may any character or action be classified as good or bad. The slaying of Oswald would have as much claim to our sympathies as the slaying of Cordelia seems to have, since to be as duteous to the vices of one's mistress "as badness would desire" is, in the absence of any set of values, every bit as defensible as devotion of an honorable daughter to her father.

Not only has a "chaotic world," as the underlying truth of reality, no meaning; it contradicts the very means of establishing *un*reason as truth. A logical and ordered analysis may conclude that logic and order do not exist in a given situation, but *only* on the presumption that they exist elsewhere and could exist here if circumstances were different. Reason cannot be used to deny reason altogether, nor can horror presuppose a norm.[28] Any dreadful act will show to what extent men may violate the good, but not that all men are essentially evil, any more than a good act means that all men are perfect.

Philosophical implications of Cordelia's death, if I may refer to them as such, lead to a mass of absurdities and contradictions—which, I dare say, are not out of place in a disordered universe. It really does not help much to say, as some have said, that the cosmic disorder of *Lear* is not necessarily Shakespeare's philosophy, since other tragedies of his have a more solidly religious basis. It is *Lear* we are discussing, and my only purpose in bringing in analogies from other plays is to show that the same arguments can be applied to them as to this, but *not* to try to conclude that, because *Hamlet,* say, or *Macbeth* is Christian, *Lear* must also be Christian since they are by the same author. However, to take *Lear* by itself does not mean that we drift involuntarily into a philosophy that is characteristic of this play only. We suspend *dis*belief when we come to the theatre, not belief, and if I honestly found the world of *Lear* to be meaningless I could not accept the play as a great tragedy. I am firmly convinced that the world of *Lear* is a very meaningful one, and the most powerful argument I can find to support this contention is the play itself.

But first we must put to rest those despairing and pessimistic analyses upon which certain modern scholars so strenuously insist. What happens in *Lear* bears undeniable likeness to what some writers of our day portray as "grotesque"; the similarities are often striking. Some writers have actually been influenced by the play. Jan Kott has a detailed essay on this subject, and one of his conclusions is that the grotesque in *King Lear,* i.e., the massive downfall of order and the utter meaninglessness of absolutes, is the message it has for our time. However, one does not read very far before seeing where Kott's essay goes wrong and how far it goes wrong:

> All bonds, all laws, whether divine, natural or human, are broken. Social order, from the kingdom to the family, will crumble into dust. There are no longer kings and subjects, fathers and children, husbands and wives. There are only huge Renaissance monsters, devouring one another like beasts of prey.[29]

Now this is manifestly untrue. Whatever dispute Kott has with the older philosophy, or whatever concessions he makes to it, not all laws are broken in *King Lear.* Not all bonds are dissolved. Not all the characters are "devouring one another like beasts of prey." When Lear banishes Cordelia he disclaims all his paternal care, propinquity and property of blood, and from that moment holds her as a stranger to his heart and him forever. Thus does the highest authority in the land pronounce sentence, rendering it the more impressive with the most solemn oaths imaginable in a pagan setting. Yet the bond remains. And Lear is just as authoritative when he banishes Kent a few moments later. Yet *that* bond remains, despite the unimpeachable power that would break it and despite the injustice that would alienate a lesser man for all future time. Edgar remains loyal to his father in a similar kind of situation. The bond between Albany and Goneril is indeed broken but it is broken by Goneril, not Albany. And whom, might I ask, are Albany, Kent, Gloucester, Edgar, Cordelia and the fool devouring "like beasts of prey"?

The world of *King Lear,* it is true, is a dreadfully upset world in which viciousness is rampant. Those who attempt to describe it can hardly find words to do so, and often resort to superlatives and exaggeration. It is a very shallow observation, however, that what is so visibly active represents all reality as the play portrays it and leaves us with a world similar to the one which Matthew Arnold sums up in the closing lines of "Dover Beach":

> Hath really neither joy, nor love, nor light,
> Nor certitude, nor peace, nor help for pain;
> And we are here as on a darkling plain
> Swept with confused alarms of struggle and flight,
> Where ignorant armies clash by night.

A forlorn drama in which this were the literal truth would be highly revealing if placed beside the *Tragedy of King Lear.* Visualize a bloody war between contesting powers that are both degenerate, or a clash of ignorance with ignorance where the struggle nought availeth—for nothing good can come out of it—and we will see more precisely just what it is that horrifies us in *King Lear.* Nothing grips us like the struggle between good and evil. Evil matched against evil is trash by comparison. Whether Goneril or Regan succeeds in winning Edmund does not engage our dramatic interest in the least. Their malicious rivalry is typical of what they are, nothing more, and the miserable ends to which they come touch us not with pity. Edmund's death is "but a trifle here."

But if Cordelia had only lived! The ejaculation escapes from everyone who has touched the very heart of the drama, regardless of what opinions he holds as to the universe above her, and demonstrates a kinship between believer and unbeliever. The distress of all of us is a measure of our belief in what she was, how much she deserved to live, and the good she might yet have accomplished. So much may be granted, that good and evil do not cease to have meaning simply because the good are killed off, yet leave the question unanswered as to the efficacy of good when it comes to such a tragic finish. Why does Cordelia die?

This problem has vexed many. Pure chance and inexplicable conduct seem to have so much to do with it that, as with much else that happens in King Lear, the effect appears grossly out of proportion to the cause. To say that such things happen in life will not do. We seek a more poetic reason. The very circumstances that lead up to her death by hanging, while they might have some place in a Hardy novel, seem like a mass of incongruous trifles amid the deeper realities of good and evil. No one on stage knows of Edmund's execution order other than Edmund himself. He and Edgar fight, and Edmund falls mortally wounded. Yet almost a hundred lines go by before he says:

> Some good I mean to do,
> Despite of mine own nature. Quickly send—
> Be brief in it—to the castle, for my writ
> Is on the life of Lear and on Cordelia.
> Nay, send in time.

Why this delay? Even when Kent comes on and mentions his master, and Albany says, "Great thing of us forgot!" another eight lines go by, during which Edmund pauses to reflect, "Yet Edmund was beloved."

First of all, the deeper realities are not so removed from this chain of events as would at first appear. Cordelia's death is planned and perpetrated by Edmund for much the same reason that Goneril and Regan plot to kill their father, and is as dramatically important as Iago's plot against the innocent newlyweds in *Othello*. Not the plot to kill Cordelia, but the effort to save her seems debased by the intervention of strange delays or forgetfulness or whatever would best explain the lapse of time when seconds are important.[30]

There are two answers to this. Till the moment that Albany challenges Edmund, the latter seems to be completely successful in everything he has so carefully planned. He *is* Earl of Gloucester. Both royal princesses are vying for his affections. He has defeated the French army and has sent the order for the deaths of Lear and Cordelia, each a potential barrier to his ultimate and unlimited power. However, the sudden appearance of an unknown champion, who pronounces him traitor and dares him to trial by combat, now stands in his way. Edmund fights bravely, be it said, as perhaps who would not who has so much within his grasp?

As his adversary's sword drives home and Edmund lies mortally wounded, all his dreams, at the very moment of being realized, are blasted, and he lies dazed with defeat and physical pain. Such a stunning reversal does not permit his thoughts to be as ordered as we would like them to be. Eleven lines go by before he speaks at all. Understand that in examining the facts as we have them, I am merely showing that the death of Cordelia is dramatically acceptable, which is a very different thing from lessening its terrible effect. The death of Duncan is dramatically acceptable, though frightful to contemplate—even in the eyes of his murderer.

Edmund fights and loses. But suppose he had won. Suppose, should he then have to fight Albany, he were to defeat *him* and thus remove the last obstacle to his ambitions. This double possibility is a very real one. Edmund would then be supreme in the land. The fate of

Lear and Cordelia would be sealed from any attempt to save them, and what further evil Edmund would perpetrate we can only conjecture. Such an outcome is prevented, of course, though not purely by chance. The one who wields the better sword, in the psychological view of Shakespeare's age and our own, is he who fights in a good cause, the only difference being that we apply the argument to war only whereas the age of Shakespeare extended it to individual combat as well. Albany's comment is pertinent:

> Where I could not be honest,
> I never yet was valiant.

To what extent the guilty conscience of Edmund is instrumental in his defeat we cannot say exactly, though the notion is common enough in other plays. Richard III, Macbeth and others suffer from the guilt they bear, and their downfall is due at least partially to it. Edmund's frank confession as he lies bleeding is an indication that he too carried a burden when he was obliged to fight.[31]

The workings of his mind do not bring him to a total and immediate conversion, which would not be likely. Somehow the realization that he too was loved seems to inspire in him a belated effort to do some good. This realization that he is loved, however, must be attributed to the moment in which he speaks it rather than simply to love itself. He knew prior to this that the two sisters hotly desired him, there being a love scene with each and a later soliloquy in which he debates the knotty problem of which one he can take. Being loved by either one meant no more to him than another opportunity to achieve power. Now, at the very moment of death, he has reason to reflect upon his past life and to recall what, if anything, has some meaning in it. Significantly, it is not his ambition, to which he devoted all his time and effort and which came very close to being realized, but the fact that he was *loved*. If all this be true, we can presume in Edmund's mind a complete disorganization of the philosophy to which he held for so long, and an emergence of new values. To be even the least bit realistic, we must allow time for all this to happen, particularly since it is not until the dead bodies of Goneril and Regan are brought before him that he realizes the intensity of their love—such as it was:

> The one the other poisoned for my sake,
> And after slew herself.

All of this is assuredly more meaningful than "pure accident" or "inexplicable delay."

I said that there are two answers to the criticism of Cordelia's death as dramatically unacceptable, and the second of these is, I believe, more important than the first. The very element of *chance,* which we cannot eliminate entirely, is itself meaningful. He who trusts to evil cannot foresee the twists and turns of events that will follow, nor can he measure the consequences of even a minor incident. It may be that the good are equally blind to the future. But the effects of one as measured against the effects of the other—certainly the play makes this clear—tend overwhelmingly toward the chaotic in the one case and toward order and stability in the other.

In our own time we hear a great deal about "overreaction," as if there were something wildly inordinate and incomprehensible about it. Actually it is almost a rule of life that evil, or even carelessness, will have results far more devastating than the act which begot them. If for no other reason that the practical one, any code of social order should take into consideration the unforeseen perils that attend the most carefully planned evil, and tragedy is well within its province in dramatizing the consequences where codes are disregarded. When Edmund gave the execution order, he thought no more about it. Who could say at the time that a very short while later (in the same scene) he will regret this order and attempt to stop its being carried out, only to have the attempt come too late? And Cordelia is victim in this unhappy chain of events! A few moments more and she might have been spared.

Returning to our question as to what precisely may be the efficacy of heroic virtue, we may concede the large results of evil yet wonder what comes of being good. Does Cordelia's death establish an immutable principle, even within the confines of Lear's own world, that, though the good would have been preferable, it is brought to naught by the forces which villainy sets in motion? Efficacy may mean many things to many people. One asks, "What can virtue accomplish?" Another asks, "What will virtue procure for the one who practices it?" Reflect well on these two questions. They are not difficult ones, nor have they hidden meanings. But they proceed from two attitudes, looking in very different directions, and we must follow each to its ultimate conclusion if we are to see the true significance of what is being asked. If we do that, if indeed we go only a portion of the way, we will wonder how the two could ever have been interpreted as asking the same thing.

Yet a great deal of what has been written on *King Lear* seems to have ignored the difference. "What good is virtue?" as I interpret the negative answers given, appears to mean, not what will virtue achieve, but what worldly profit can it expect. Cosmic chaos as well as chaos in the world of men are both presumed from an evident failure of the good to find the reward they have merited (as for punishing the evil, there is no doubt whatever that the evil are punished). Since the afterlife is ruled out as irrelevant to secular drama, or what is called secular drama, death must be seen as the end of everything and not as a passage into eternity. Consequently, the happy ending in Tate's version would, from a strictly secular point of view, be preferable: Cordelia is saved, she and Edgar accept each other in love, Lear is restored to his kingdom, and the moral of the play is given in the closing lines:

> Thy bright example shall convince the world
> (Whatever storms of fortune are decreed)
> That truth and vertue shall at last succeed.

Those who would have preferred the happy ending can, of course, disavow these lines on the ground that they are Tate's, not Shakespeare's, but had Shakespeare himself written two endings, one tragic and one happy, and left it up to posterity to decide between them, I believe the choice would be heavily in favor of the tragic ending, though both were in Shakespeare's very best style. There are meanings in the tragic version almost too vast to be recognized, though we sense their presence, and we cannot dodge them by damning Tate unmercifully. Our decision must be based on something more than style.

To begin with, the secular approach is decidedly out of keeping with the age in which *King Lear* was written, and actually presumes more than the religious interpretation does. I do not mean that the Elizabethan age was solid and uniform in its acceptance of Christian teachings. We know that much Renaissance thinking went far in its denial of Christian tenets, and Elton's book does a valuable service in examining so thoroughly and documenting so carefully this new thought.[32] But all that Elton can really do is suggest the possibility that *Lear* might be interpreted according to the new thought, essentially on two grounds: (1) that such thought had gained acceptance in many quarters and (2) that the action of the play would seem to conform to it rather than to medieval Christianity. We must remember, however, that medieval Christianity was also very much alive and much more widely accepted than the new rationalism. One large portion of Elton's scholarship establishes this fact. He cites many contemporary writers who complained about the new anti-Christian teachings and who wrote answers to it, sometimes very spirited answers, thereby demonstrating how widespread this new thought must have been. But these answers and complaints indicate as well that there was a strong body of opinion still committed to the old way. Background scholarship is always valuable, but it can only aid, it cannot determine, the meaning of a literary work.

The terms *religious play* and *secular play* are a little too rigidly applied, as if one were a different species altogether from the other. To what extent either would apply to *King Lear* is lost in the exclusiveness by which many understand *religious* and *secular,* and I would prefer to drop both along with all the bans and prohibitions they have managed to pick up from popular usage. I mention the Christianity of the Elizabethan-Jacobean age merely to caution the secularists of our own time against ruling out what they regard as extraneous to the domain of drama. Contemporary thought definitely favors the rational as opposed to the Christian, and if we must all be warned against allowing "fondness for our own philosophical beliefs" to determine our view of Shakespeare, the warning might better be given to the rationalist or the nihilist than to the Christian.

Now, as far as Christianity is concerned, the value of the good life is measured in terms of what it will accomplish for others rather than what it will reap for itself. The most basic Christian teachings stress this over and over again. The ideal Chrisitian is he who sacrifices all, even to the extremity of laying down his life for his friend or for his beliefs, whereas reward, if it has been merited, will be given in a supernatural existence to follow this one. The principle is clear, almost hackneyed from repetition.

The death of Cordelia involves a certain mystery, not in the sense that it is completely beyond our power to understand, but rather because it involves realities that are only partially within our ken. But so does the death of Christ, the deaths of the early martyrs, indeed the death of many a sacrificial victim who is executed for political or other principles in which he happens to believe. Whether the early martyrs were put to death because they were regarded as subversive or merely to provide sport for spectators in the arena really makes no difference. Their beliefs rather than the more practical reasons of their killers are the determining factor. To Edmund, Cordelia was simply a threat to his political aspirations, and if he thought at all about her good qualities he probably dismissed them as a piece of silliness, not unlike his father's astrology. To look at it from Cordelia's point of view, she has come on a mission to save her father. The possibility of military defeat and capture (both of which come to pass) was something she had to risk from the very beginning. Consequently, the goodness she extends to the King who wronged her is no mere comfortable giving from her bounty as Queen of France. She has to invade a country which, though the land of her birth, is now alien, and she must be prepared to face whatever consequences will follow. It is in the pursuit of this valiant endeavor that she meets her death.

These considerations, it is true, do not materially enlighten us on the actual circumstances of the deed in question. Her hanging takes place off stage, so that we do not see her die, and the manner in which she meets her death we can only presume from her character generally and the way in which she has met other reverses heretofore. When disowned and banished by her father, she reacted with quiet courage and with tears, exhibiting anything but the "coldness" sometimes attributed to her. Again when her army was defeated in battle and she and her father were taken prisoner, she behaved with calm resignation to what must have been one of the supreme disappointments of her life:

> We are not the first
> Who with best meaning have incurred the worst.
> For thee, oppressed King, am I cast down.
> Myself could else outfrown false fortune's frown.

If we can assume anything at all, it is that she met her death in much the same way, and this accords, I believe, with the larger view of tragic meaning, as I have attempted to set if forth, rather than with the mere frustration of worldly hopes—powerful though that might be. To condemn the slaying of Cordelia, as we certainly must, we are obliged to condemn it on a moral basis, and when we do that we imply foundations of the "good" that transcend the successes and failures of this life.

The death of Cordelia does not differ in any material way from the other sacrificial deaths. The power of Shakespeare's art simply makes it more vivid. Not through ghastly details does Shakespeare work nor through any means that would horrify only by degrading, but rather through what he has achieved in the character he has created and through the love he has inspired for her. Far from contradicting the meaning of Christian sacrifice, this brutal hanging is an insight into the very heart of it. Behold that lifeless body, feel the pangs as Lear must feel them, and then know what it means to have the guiltless suffer for the crimes of the guilty. Till now, you may have thought tales of martyrs to be nothing more than pretty stories for children. But if the dead Cordelia incites you to call the universe insane, your emotion is understandable, for you are seeing sacrifice—truly *seeing* it—for the first time.

IX

THE DEATH OF LEAR

The supreme sacrifice which love has made is now the burden Lear holds in his arms. The anguish he feels is the final and ultimate reduction of authority before the power of love whose bond, expressed earlier in terms that seemed almost to belittle it, is greater than all else. Broken, distracted, pitiful, Lear sobs out the question:

> Why should a dog, a horse, a rat, have life
> And thou no breath at all? Thou'lt come no more,
> Never, never, never, never, never!

The "unrelieved tragedy" of this final scene must be viewed as nothing less and must be interpreted in the strictest relationship of what has gone before. No death scene in Shakespeare could really mean very much if we were seeing the tragic characters for the first time, but the dramatic metamorphosis of *King Lear* is something far more important than mere acquaintance with principles. Hardly could we see the "unrelieved tragedy" in its almost divine setting if we have grown forgetful of the central actor. As there have been many who failed to recognize a certain stateliness in the Lear who presided as King over the court of Britain, so there have been many—frequently the same ones—who fail to see him now as a man utterly destitute of former greatness, and what precisely the change means.

Between the former Lear and the present one there is such a difference that we can hardly believe them to be the same man. A Lear in absolute command of himself and others, as we have seen him at the beginning—and his sin is the more serious for that—is a Lear whose pronouncements we analyze and judge from a strictly philosophical or moral point of view. A Lear crushed by the tragedy of the daughter whose inestimable goodness he has finally come to know is in the grip of something more powerful than authority and more lasting than life itself. The tragedy can be traced entirely to evil causes and is not a chance occurrence in the haphazard conflict of chaotic forces. Its result is more terrible than, it does not contradict, a conventional belief that evil stems from evil and good stems from good. Tragedy, as I have already stated, does not of itself disprove the order of the universe; it is simply a violation of that order, and is meaningful *only* when seen in relation to the order it violates.

The role which Lear himself plays, however, involves two important considerations that prompt a pessimistic view of the world in which he lives, considerations which are more often sensed than carefully isolated and thought upon. One I have already mentioned in the preceding chapter: the penitence and purification of Lear that would appear to forecast a happy reclamation of the sinner. The other is the alleged "despair" at the moment of death.

To return to the first of these. Lear's reunion with Cordelia is indeed complete in a much more perfect way than if his frustration, brought on by her death, were to come about through some other means. Let us imagine her proving unworthy of the pedestal on which she has stood for so long, or luring her father into sentimentalities of affection only to laugh in his face and take a revenge most bitter to contemplate. "If you have poison for me, I will drink it," he tells her, and so he might have done. If, as he thinks, she has "some cause" not to love him, the mild vengeance of remaining cool to him would be natural. But vengeance of any kind is completely foreign to her character, certainly the unthinkable vengeance of deliberately assuming a pretense of love so as to disarm the penitent father and thereby wound him the more savagely. No such thing happens. Cordelia remains pure to the end. Whatever theories may tend to prove the universe to be chaotic, there is one that is notably absent: the progress of a repentant sinner toward that which appears to be love and turns out to be hate. Death may frustrate, but it does not corrupt. Loves stays constant and achieves in death a mystical nobility that we can no longer think of in worldly terms. If the reunion of Lear and Cordelia is to grow into this kind of love, it must do so in another life.

Faith in such an outcome is given to more men than is generally believed. But Lear is not one of them, and when we reflect upon the age in which he lived we are not surprised. It is an era of paganism in which the gods have, at best, some vague connection with human affairs and are appealed to only at moments of crisis or high emotion. No religious philosophy is apparent anywhere, barring a certain kind of natural ethics which presumably has divine favor. In such an age we can hardly look for anything like complete resignation to the will of a just but unfathomable deity. Lear's "religious" attitude, so-called, is a part of him and deserves to be noted. It is not, however, a major part, and it subserves rather than controls the more prominent aspects of his character. Knight is quite correct in his comment that the gods in *Lear* are natural rather than supernatural; one feels them to be figments of the human mind rather than omnipotent ruling powers. After citing many references to the gods, Knight concludes: "These phrases do not form a convincing declaration of divine reality: some show at the most an insistent need in humanity to cry for justification to something beyond its horizon, others are almost perfunctory."[33]

It is true that occasionally Lear's invocations of the gods are more than casual ones and would seem to suggest a somewhat more than passive belief. When he banishes Cordelia, for instance, he says:

> . . . by the sacred radiance of the sun,
> The mysteries of Hecate, and the night,
> By all the operation of the orbs
> From whom we do exist and case to be,
> Here I disclaim all my paternal care . . .

Later, however, he banishes Kent for seeking to make him change his decision. The reasons Lear gives have nothing to do with the sacredness of any vow, either to the gods or to nature, but concern exclusively his position and place:

> Since thou hast sought to make us break our vow,
> Which we durst never yet, and with strained pride
> To come between our sentence and our power—
> Which nor our nature nor our place can bear,
> Our potency made good—take thy reward.

"*I* have spoken" is the substance of this, rather than "I am bound by the powers above."

To concede and at the same time discountenance the view that the play is set in a pagan age and would not therefore apply to a Christian one is an attempt to run the argument both ways and thereby avoid a glaring difficulty. Nor will the argument of "parallels" or "analogy" help much. A faith in the supernatural, a belief in the ultimate goodness of things are, be it admitted, parallels of what Christians essentially believe. Consequently, we are asked to conclude, the chaotic tragedy, while tactfully placed in a pagan world, applies equally to all ages and is very easily translated.

But is it? We cannot escape so easily from the very

conditions of Lear's beliefs. There is nothing in his pagan background which would have taught him to accept his downfall with patience and to trust in a merciful God who will welcome him into His kingdom. Precisely what religious teaching is Lear disobeying? The natural man reacting to his noblest instincts in rediscovering the love he once cast off is grief-stricken at its loss. The grief, regardless of how it is expressed, is but a measure of the love he feels and is not to be taken as his philosophy of life. We can go so far as to say that he suffers the same pangs a saint would feel under similar circumstances, without the supernatural light given to the saint to teach him their meaning. Lear cannot, therefore, be judged guilty. The meaning lies in what happens to him, not in his understanding of it, for the road he travels and the origin of his sorrows are exactly the same as those of the religiously enlightened. May the ignorant be saved as well, if like Lear, they have fallen and repented according to such intuition as they happen to possess? The mystery is deliberately set forth and the answer is suggested, as we shall see, in as inscrutable a way as the question we ask.

Lear's anguish, since we make additional allowance for the fact that he is not completely in his right mind, is not only understandable but dramatically defensible. Those who maintain a steadfast faith in the image of Cordelia, whose life they cannot regard as meaningless on account of its untimely end, will not shy away from the impact of her death. They will stress it to the full. What she was in life cannot be separated from it. The more we increase the one the more we must increase the other as well. It is a great deal to ask of the pagan Lear, that he, bowed as he is under the inseparable combination, should calmly view each one by itself and remain conscious of victory rather than of defeat. A triumphant Lear would violate not only all naturalness and likelihood but a serious dramatic fact, and we should be honest with ourselves whether we fully appreciate his sorrow yet expect him to master it, or whether we simply want a softening of the tragic tone in order to ease our own feelings. It is certainly easier to bear another's afflictions, no matter how severe they may be, when they are locked safely inside. Sympathy, such as that which we feel for the man who has disowned his daughter and refuses to speak of her, may search out the anguish beneath the calm exterior and feel a sincere admiration for him who suffers in silence.

Now, however, Lear is utterly broken. His last vestige of strength is gone. Completely overwhelmed with sorrow, he gives vent to an unstemmed flow of bitter emotion.

It is a question as to how effectively the virtuous character may be portrayed in its fullest meaning—the fulfillment of dramatic comedy or the frustration of tragedy. The profoundest effect comes in the destruction, not in the having, of what we most cherish. A paradox this may be, but one of constant proof. To have and to lose, to wish for and be denied, establishes a sense of value that possession cannot equal—unless one is gifted with the grace of vividly fictionalizing the loss of what he wants to continue to enjoy. "What would life be like without you?" The question is not uncommon, and if asked in all seriousness it may heighten our appreciation considerably of the one we love. In the sublimity of high tragedy we undergo something like the actual experience and return to life with cleaner vision. Regardless of how true all this may be for us, however, the question remains as to whether the one who suffers bereavement is simply the unfortunate sacrifice for our betterment or, all else presumed to be right, he undergoes a purgation more sublime than ours.

King Lear suffers, not because some have read Christianity into it, but because others have read Christianity *out* of it. Many have been deeply moved by the play without necessarily thinking of it as Christian. It is when we insist on its being categorically *un*christian or anti-christian that we begin to confuse its meaning and misread its characters. More philosophies that Christianity have a stake in *Lear*, in that they too would see merit in a story of expiation, forgiveness, reconciliation and an ultimate purification of the one who did wrong. Certainly there is a direction in which the play appears to be moving—this cannot be denied—and which alone causes disagreement as to what the end may mean. We are led to expect something which apparently never comes to pass, or a goal is set up which is snatched away at the very moment it is attained. Had Lear never repented of his sin, had he remained just as adamant as he was when he replied to the Duke of Burgundy, "I have sworn, I am firm," we would accept his tragic end as naturally as we accept the downfall of Macbeth. But Macbeth grows constantly worse as a result of what he did. Lear grows better. He is an altogether different person at the end from what he was at the beginning. We cannot argue away certain elements of punishment, atonement, enlightenment and repentance, whether or not we accept in our final analysis the purgatorial interpretation. It is this apparent conflict, rather than the total absence, which is the real point at issue.

By denying the play a "happy ending," Shakespeare is simply excluding one kind of fulfillment—the worldly one—and leaving the other open. It is unfair to say that he excludes both. Keeping in mind the dramatic progress of the story and the pagan background of its protagonist, we must see the very theme of enlightenment, if it is to make any sense, as presupposing the ignorance it is come to dispel. From the beginning of the play what happens to Lear is more than he can understand. Not a saint upon a quest who follows the beacon light of his own faith, Lear stumbles about in darkness and is the recipient of the action rather than its determiner; or, to complete the analogy, the suffering which a saint might bear with patient fortitude Lear responds to with instincts that are wholly natural and human. Is not his experience a way of discovering what the saint already knows? Knowledge such as this imposes a fearful duty, from which, happily, Lear is free. How, then, can it be said that he *despairs,* a word that, even in its secular sense, would have to presume a knowledge he never had?

When we consider the power and might of this drama as well as the purport it leads us to discover, we cannot avoid the question: Is Lear being prepared for death? To put it a better way: Is he being prepared for life or for eternity? To what does the purification of Lear lead? The happy ending, pleasant as it may be, is simply inadequate. We seek some meaning beyond a peaceful restructuring of what has been torn assunder.

Queer that those who talk of cosmic significance where it has no real connection should have missed it in the very place we ought to seek it. This is the final consummation of all. Our choice must be between two totally opposite extremes: complete downfall or resurrection. In choosing between infinity and zero, we would, without incurring the charge of prejudice or narrowness, find the first of these more in keeping with the story. But facts either continue to support our choice or prove worthless as any valid argument against it.

In laboring to prove the despair of Lear, Elton bases his conclusions on two essential points: Lear pronounces his daughter gone from him forever, thus denying the after-life, and he seeks — without finding — some signs of life in her; he dies, not in ecstasy as Bradley thought, but in despair.[34] Gloucester, says Elton, dies between two extremes: grief and joy. But the extremes in Lear are hope and despair, with the latter winning at the very moment of death.

This reading, however, misses entirely what is actually uppermost, the grief of a distraught father, in preference for a literal interpretation of the words spoken. I might point out that Lear calls those who are on stage, i.e., Kent, Albany, Edgar and others, "murderers, traitors all." Are we to assume from this that Lear is expressing a considered opinion that these others are accessory to Cordelia's death? As many a true word is spoken in jest, so many a false word is spoken in high emotion, and it is emotion that is more likely to be sincere. How separate the true from the untrue, the sincere from the insincere? It can and must be done, both in life and in masterworks of fiction that probe all the conflicts and disturbances of the human mind. Nothing is to be gained from rigid simplicities: "He said it, he meant it, and we judge him accordingly." The sympathy of those whom he accuses is closer to the truth. They behold their King mad with grief, unburdening his soul in bitter condemnation of all who might have saved his daughter instead of, as he sees them, just standing around and doing nothing. How they might have saved Cordelia is difficult to imagine, nor do we impute to Lear any real belief that they could have done so.

Yet it makes as much sense to take these words seriously as it does to put a literal interpretation on other poignant expressions of Lear's broken heart. Grief at the death of a loved one, we are asked to assume, is contradictory to a belief in the afterlife. Instead of the pagan Lear, however, take any Christian father and imagine him going through the same experience through which Lear goes. Picture him viewing his dead daughter and try to imagine what his feelings would be. Only the worst of cynics would casually point out that the father's sorrow constitutes a denial of his religious tenets. "Gone forever" is an ejaculation of terrible distress, and many a sincere Christian has said it, with no thought whatever of denying life after death. The grief of Lear is the matter of this scene, not his religious philosphy.

The closing lines of the play clearly point up the fact

that intense emotion will almost necessarily differ from a more deeply pondered analysis of what life means:

> The weight of this sad time we must obey,
> Speak what we feel, not what we ought to say.

How many have considered the deep meaning of these lines? What is the difference between "what we feel" and "what we ought to say"? The stress on *feel* and *ought* suggests, even in the heart of the cultured pagan, a contrast between the present horrors and a sense of duty, the one overwhelming the other only in obedience to the weight of this sad time and not as a permanent displacement of it. There is a difference but not a contradiction, and we must insist on one as firmly as we deny the other. The sad time will pass. At a later date it will be easier to speak "what we ought to say." But, looking back upon the tragedy to which they were all witness, no one will conclude that his expression of sorrow was wrong or in any way compromised a persisting faith in something better.

As regards the words right at Lear's death, Battenhouse makes an exceedingly significant point when he stresses the mystery that is evident in Lear's very last speech:[35]

> Do you see this? Look on her, look, her lips,
> Look there, look there!

What is it that Lear sees? Too many people, says Battenhouse, have assumed that Lear sees, or thinks he sees, signs of natural life in Cordelia. Is it really this, or is it something else? The words do not tell us, and their very obscurity is striking, coming as it does at the moment that Lear himself dies. The conjecture, the mystery, the question as to what happens after death, all of which has apparently been ruled out as beyond the scope and concern of drama, seems deliberately posed by the author himself.

It is not simply that the meaning is unknown. A word or two might have clarified it. Yet Shakespeare chose to be mysterious, and mystery, like silence, may simply be absence of meaning, or it may, if it comes at a climactic moment toward which all else points, indicate something infinitely beyond our power to know or express. The sublime heights Shakespeare's poetry has reached breathe of but an earthly world. But what a world it is! *Cosmic,* though a term often used incorrectly when speaking of this world of *Lear,* comes unbidden to the tongue. And what small beginnings it seems to have had, if we miss the true importance of that test of love which brought it all forth! Even if we realize the deep relationship between love and order, we are still amazed at the magnitude of what follows. What more can man envision than the vastness of the good and of the evil portrayed in the mighty conflict? What choices did the dramatist have from which he might select an appropriate conclusion? The downfall of everything: all has been meaningless, as Edmund informed us long ago, and the answer is simply that there is no answer? The happy ending: the mouse labored and brought forth a mountain, which somehow gets back into the mouse? Shakespeare saw that only death could conclude such a story as this, but death that means something infinitely more than tragic doom.

Good impulses and bad began all this action. Those concerned could not foresee the titanic convulsions that would come of what they did. When all the turmoil is ended, there is no return to the apparent insignificance of the opening scene; in fact there is no return at all. The ever widening progress continues—into eternity!

In the cluster of figures that stand about the dead King there is the strongest evidence that the world of *Lear* is not a chaotic one. The atmosphere is grim rather than hopeless. The power of evil, not the power of good, has been utterly destroyed. The play has demonstrated that evil is potent, that it may inflict much harm on the innocent and win many victories, but that it will not survive. Though given everything that the world could possibly label as success and happiness, the wicked could discover no basis for amity and continuance; they were a house divided. It is *their* bonds that are broken. The bond between the dead Lear and his followers remains firm. No bond among the evil characters was at any time as strong as that which exists now between the living and the dead.

Shakespearean creation has, if we are to judge from the history of commentary on his plays, been a conflict between poetic insight and conscious artistry, two methods that do not always resolve themselves into a Hegelian synthesis. Poetic insight has brought to life King Lear, Cordelia, Kent, Edmund, Edgar, Gloucester, and all the others, making them as real and vivid as one could wish, perhaps more real than many actual people with whom we are intimately acquainted. So much will be granted for poetic insight. What of conscious artistry? Is the drama formed and the action controlled so as to produce what we would call a "good play"? With a poet so imaginative as Shakespeare, the tendency has been to see him as excessively strong in one respect and careless in the other—poetic power, to switch metaphors, becomes an unmanageable steed that carries its rider whither it will. On this precise issue much criticism is leveled at *King Lear*. The characters are a success, but the play is—well, if not a failure, certainly a loosely knit and poorly motivated story with powerful poetry and vivid characterization. This opinion never seemed to me to have any validity, though I concede the natural conflict between inspiration and the rules of art. What if insight should penetrate to truth in a way not beyond our understanding but certainly beyond our power to duplicate?

In looking philosphically at the life of his time, Henry Adams wondered whether there could be a "larger synthesis" that would join all the divergent forces which seemed to exist only in themselves and to be moving ever farther and farther apart.[36] A similar question poses itself regarding *King Lear*. Are all the characters merely the unrelated creatures of intense poetic inspiration, moving away from one another according to their respective individualities and serving no dramatic purpose other than to become more completely alive? If this is how the play came to be written, the tragic end may be nothing more then a convenience. Characters in fiction have frequently been killed off when the author did not know what else to do with them, or found that he had exhausted all his inventiveness and must simply stop writing. In such cases we look in vain for a comprehensive whole, much as we admire the individual parts. If this problem exists in *King Lear,* Nahum Tate has solved it by giving us, not a "higher synthesis," but a lower one. Characters move apart and come back together again. The world that was shattered is reassembled in something like its original form. In Shakespeare, however, the very centers of the old world are destroyed. Lear, the point upon which all love and loyalty converges, now lies dead. Cordelia, who represents true and enduring love, lies dead beside him.

The burning question naturally keeps recurring: in probing deeply into characters so rich and varied as those in *King Lear,* is the dramatist necessarily involved in a separate quest with each? Does every path lead away from every other path as all become more individualized, with the result that the more thoroughly the particular character is delineated the less can the entire cast be made to act according to some plan, artistic or otherwise, that will involve them all? Or is there, deep within the soul of each, a discoverable synthesis—not without complexities of its own—that achieves the function of that shallower conformity the lesser dramatist imposes, though in a way far more profound? If there is, what better medium can there be than a civilization blasted into a turmoil of discoveries about itself?

I am far from suggesting that these questions have never been dealt with before. But I believe there is a distinct bias among the critics toward the lower synthesis rather than the higher one, which is very surprising, since it is the lower one they dislike. When life and character are interpreted according to some quite evident philosophy, such as Christianity, the cry of "morality play" is heard on all sides, the epithet being intended in its most damning sense, and we are told that the story is made to conform to a particular view. Such a work is little better than propaganda. Life is not like that.

On the other hand, a truly complex work of art is said to have no special creed at the heart of it—the statement has often been made about Shakespeare himself—and characters, art, life and heaven knows what else are all emancipated simply by being what they are and conforming to no constricting dogmas. Life's variations, in other words, are not subject to interpretation. If art is to imitate life it must be similarly free of anything that would impose standards or criteria according to which we form our judgments.

Now, it cannot be said that *King Lear* or any other work of literature is free in any such sense as this, i.e., that there are no constricting boundaries such as critics complain of in other works, and that the "free" action of varied characters eludes every plan of life, all principle of order and any indication that divine justice is concerned with the affairs of men. If we look deeply into the heart of each evil character, we shall read a terrible condemnation of his hypotheses and the actions that result from them. We shall have a similar, though opposite, reaction to the good. The death of the innocent Cordelia we shall deplore, according to the very morality which many insist we rejected at the outset. The synthesis that involves them all is vaster and much more inclusive than their varied types would seem to admit. I am convinced that if Shakespeare had written the play with no thought of art at all, he would have discovered within the depths of his characters the very principles we assign exclusively to art—or to morality.

This may be an assumption, but rejection must assume as much as acceptance does. The play must be our guide. As Lear survives in that mysterious life to which he has gone, in another sense he survives in the life he has left. There is an emblem of authority every bit as manifest here as in the royal Lear at the beginning of the play, and it is the more impressive amid the ruination with which the play closes. Visualize the splendor of one and the starkness of the other, and reflect deeply on what it is that has remained constant from that scene to this.

What we are confronted with is truly a higher synthesis. If Lear and Cordelia had been merely father and daughter we might not be seeking the meaning that is so stoutly affirmed and stoutly denied. Unlike other tragedies, this one cannot be viewed simply as the downfall and death of protagonist. The world picture we are left with transcends the individual character, and while this is partially accounted for by extending the action into a double plot, each story traverses the same long road of suffering and expiation, toward heights that life cannot contain. Nothing in the play is trivial. Only the appearance is. Our vision is limited by the surface beneath and the sky above, and as conflicts arise we are apt to think of practical solutions, such as tact, reasonableness, expedience. Principles concerning love and authority sound artificial and inappropriate. Only the consequences can reveal the vast depths beneath the surface and make us turn our eyes upward in search of what lies far away and beyond. What happens is dreadful to behold, but not devoid of meaning. Once we affirm this much, we cannot be satisfied with a small truth. Either it is vast or it does not exist.

If we turn back to earth and look for truth in something like the Platonic sense—that which survives, as opposed to that which exists but for a time only—we can hardly conclude that the formless chaos in *Lear* is the ultimate reality. It is mighty but it is short-lived, and when the play ends this chaos is over. Not Kent, not Edgar, not Albany is swerved one iota from the path of conscious rectitude, despite the gratuitous hardship visited upon each. A pitiful and dejected remnant they may be, but they are alive and victorious at the end. Is this nothing?

Tradition is only the first step toward, or the first glimpse of, the transcendental. As such, it is no more to be confused with mere continuation from age to age than the sincere believer is to be confused with the creature of habit, though both attend the same church. That which deserves to live on is above all the practical considerations and passing interests of a particular era. Though not everything that survives can be said to meet this qual-ification, we can best distinguish the good from the bad by the solid virtues of those who project the past into the future. Those who remain after Lear to do this are king-centered, it is true, rather than God centered. The divinities in which they believed were projections of their own personalities. The King was real. If a royal king falls short of what we conceive to be higher truth, he is the farthest point they can see with any clarity, and the direction in which they have been looking is the right one.

Lear, not Everyman, went on that journey with Death, and how much the others understood his purification and eventual condition of soul we do not know, but he went subject to higher powers and profounder laws than even he understood. All this we must leave in the mystery with which Shakespeare has enshrouded it, and turn back to dwell upon the group left standing about the dead King. It

is they who are united in something that the departed Lear
has bequeathed them. As Carlyle justly observes of Odin,
hypocrisy might have become involved with the worship of
this pagan hero, whatever he was in real life, but hypocrisy
neither began it nor could account for it. Something vital
was at its heart. The story of Lear is, happily or otherwise,
free of any implication of the "hero" in the Carlylean
sense, but it does provoke certain observations about what
we may truly label a "great man." Sham and hypocrisy,
wherever they are found, are opposed to Lear, not with
him. Nor is there any slavish addiction to royalty on the
part of his followers. Truth, love and self-sacrifice all side
with him to the very end and comprise a foundation on
which society will be rebuilt after the destruction wrought
by Lear's enemies.

Those who survive him are an incontrovertible tribute
to the King who symbolized something more than the
faults of which he was guilty, and which they saw as
clearly as anyone did. It is they who speak the final words.
All hope depends on the virtues they have practised and
the beliefs they continue to hold. Battered warriors all,
reeling from the conflict, bloody, they are more glorious in
all their devastated appearance than those whose victories
come easily and whose countenances smile in triumph.

X

EPILOGUE

It is an irony of considerable point that we can detect in so royal a play as *Lear* a principle that has bearing upon successful democracy. A government cannot long exist without moral obligations which, no matter how closely we scrutinize them, would seem to be indifferent to the strict business of government itself. I am not speaking of prohibitions, which are purely negative, nor of civic duties, but of obligations which do not proceed from any particular social pattern.

We are told that in a democracy people are, within prescribed legal limits, free to do as they please. The only way in which freedom may be modified, or specified, or more properly understood, is with respect to its ultimate limits: beyond a certain point freedom would be dangerous. So much will be granted, and if we confine our analysis to the form of government which we call democracy, there is no more to be said. The concept is complete. All religions and concepts of morality are immaterial to the fact that, whether thoroughly degraded or splendidly good, a people continues to live under a specific political arrangement, and what the individual does, if it pleases him and violates no law, is his own business. To speak, therefore, of *principle* in any other sense but the political one is to wander off into an unrelated subject.

The conviction has long existed, in fact, that democracy enjoys a peculiar kind of self-sufficiency. Royalty, at least as we see it in retrospect, may have continued in office to do good or to do bad, but the only calamity that can befall a democracy is a violation of the conditions according to which it was set up. So long as it fulfills the strict definition of what it is—that is to say, while it *lives*—it remains an autonomous, self-sufficient entity. Anything other than freedom is incidental, and becomes dangerous when taken too seriously.

This belief, somewhat convincing in the abstract, is squarely opposed to the myriad activities of any democratic population. Freedom holds a very important place, but its rank is one among many. No more than royalty is freedom deserving of blind veneration for whatever it may do, and it is certain that those who judge it by other standards are the ones who venerate it most, just as those whose "large speeches" in its behalf are deservedly suspect.

Many analyses of *Lear* which reason to a disordered universe as the ultimate reality would come to similar conclusions about the break-up of a republican form of government, provided the people concerned did not remain anonymous but were as vividly known as the major characters in *Lear*. The possibility of such a break-up is, of course, the first point in dispute, since the precise incidents in Shakespeare's tragedy could hardly take place in a democratic society. No chief executive would have the power to divide the rule among his offspring, however well thought out his original plan, much less to change his plan on the spur of the moment and in response to professions of love for his own person. Relationship between him and his daughters would have to remain a private matter, and though he might reward and disown according to such wealth as he happens to possess, his action could not have the political consequences that we see in *King Lear*.

Let us allow this advantage to democratic principles,

but only with concession that it is more misleading than enlightening. Our tendency to regard Lear's actions from the point of view of democracy strengthens our faith in the safeguards of our way of life, just as it increases our distrust of kings, who have the power to do so much harm. As we read the play we sense a disproportion between cause and effect, since, in the kind of society we have today, we are able to see disproportion in what one man does rather than in what many men do. We are wrong in both cases. The action in Shakespeare's play is brought before our eyes with painful clarity, dramatized in all its powerful psychology, and pursued to a kind of universal destruction which the forces of the good manage to survive. That the story involves relatively few people (we care little about the soldiers killed in the battle) is an advantage to the dramatist. It would be impossible to portray the same thing taking place in a representative government without a cast literally of thousands—perhaps millions. But the camouflage of numbers conceals, it does not prohibit the action.

Separation of governmental powers and the limitations imposed upon those powers merely divide the responsibility, so that, while the story of a king and his three daughters could not take place in the United States of America, power bowing to flattery most certainly could. That the play continues to appeal today is proof that this principle, though sensed rather than perfectly understood, still applies. It is completely illogical to attempt to explain its failure to reach moderns—no such failure exists!—on the ground that we on this side of the seventeenth century think as the villain of the play thought. The "we" who so think are indeed in line with Edmund's rejectionism, Goneril's emancipation from all bonds of love and duty, and Regan's animalistic determination to follow her sister's lead. How these three could have fashioned a workable democracy, how they could even be regarded as ideal members of one already in existence, is a mystery to anyone who pauses to think, and I see no evidence that modern audiences approve what Shakespeare quite obviously condemns.

All true believers in democracy will recognize instantly Edmund's dream of power. He does not desire liberty for its own sake, which, though a wrong concept of liberty, is better by far than his avowed purpose of achieving lordship for himself and subjecting others to his will. In the rebellion of Cordelia and Kent free man will find his own voice. Though these two remain loyal to that against which they are in temporary opposition, we find in their very loyalty the safest guide through the vast possibilities and incoherences of political emancipation. Cordelia's stimulus in particular lies in the virtues she prizes so highly. She is not, as sometimes she is thought to be, repelled by the life she has been forced to lead at court and, as a result, yearning to be free of it. The very basis of her filial affections is to be found in the treasure of love which her father—somewhat unwittingly—is perverting. Freedom is, for her, the opportunity to love and be loyal in the purest way.

There is nothing very abstruse about all this. The most natural reaction to the events of the play will approximate what I have just said, and even in the terms I use. It is when we begin to think more deeply upon it that we are in danger of becoming confused. Theory, spun of intellectual abstractions, assails us in an unguarded moment, not unlike Milton's serpent offering Eve something more elevated than the simple goodness she has thus far known. Liberty and virtue by themselves are perfectly compatible and reasonably safe. It is theoretical feedom and theoretical virtue that are likely to come into conflict. The ordinary man who enjoys being free and recognizes those duties which are thereby enjoined upon him will condemn Edmund as a bad man and think no more about it. Owing no deference to royalty *per se,* the less pretentious reader will nevertheless understand that people believed in it once upon a time, and he will judge character exclusively on the moral question. If we are not satisfied with this homespun philosophy, however, we cannot simply rise to the middle air which evil spirits may reach; we must go all the way beyond it to the very gates of heaven. It is here that we find the origin of true freedom and the basis for real virtue. Directly beneath is nought but speculation, which, while somewhat more elevated than the earthly, draws its inferences from below rather than from above. Just being free becomes a desideratum in itself, and indeed the only one. Whatever can be defined as *emancipation,* regardless of the sense in which we use the term, is justifiable, as anything that would impede or deny it is considered reprehensible. Bonds such as we have in *King Lear* are restrictions that it is somehow forward-looking to dissolve. The only recognizable limit to freedom is the political one—safeguarding individual rights from the criminal acts of others—and since the political system in *Lear* offers little guidance in this respect, we naturally, if we are still theorizing, dismiss the politics of Shakespeare altogether.

Consequently, as we are witnessing at the present time, a philosophy that began with a belief in political freedom ends by justifying political enslavement. The political, once severely limited in what it had power to do, becomes the sole criterion of good and bad and recognizes the worth of nothing but what lies within its scope. Though this idea too may seem highly theoretical rather than practical, facts are enlightening at every turn. The super-eminence of freedom is a declared war on all forms of obedience (except, of course, political obedience), loyalty (except political), indebtedness, idealism, perseverance (always excepting *political*). The resulting chaos among the population at large and the idolatry of a political theory combine to breed statism: problems become acute and only in government may we look for solutions. Not only is philosophical idealism regarded as trivial and impractical; it is treated as of another, and decidedly lower, order than the pressing difficulties in which man finds himself.

Insofar as we have brought this situation on ourselves, we have followed the course of Edmund's nihilism and have paved the way for his practical-minded and ambitious counterpart to grasp at power in much the same way he did. How many people today think like Edmund is a question I will not attempt to answer. Obviously not everyone does. It is as well, however, that the claim is made, though not by me: that we and Edmund think alike. Let it remain as a terrible warning.

It is much easier to condemn what is wrong than to praise what is right. Sin, failure, degradation all lend themselves to easy analysis, as if analysis itself always finds its proper meat in the wrongfulness of man. There is a deep truth somewhere in such an idea. For when we resolve to start over and to reconstruct what lies in ruins, doing our best to avoid the mistakes of the past, we are thinking too much like Edmund. We are seeking what is expedient, and are perhaps more in line with his rejection-ism that we would like to believe. We are planning to achieve something, in what seems to be the most effective way to get it. So was Edmund. The retort that he was evil is quite meaningless if all it amounts to is that his methods were self-destructive, or that what is good holds out more hope for success that evil does. Such an approach judges good and evil by their efficiency, not by any instrinsic value (or lack of it) that may be ascribed to either one. How, then, condemn Edmund for differing with us as to which is more likely to achieve the desired end? The answer is that we cannot, nor can we, if we place the same reliance on good that he placed on evil, hope for that last-minute enlightenment that came to him. Rather we are plunged into notions of a disordered universe. Good being efficient and evil inefficient, Cordelia and Lear should both be alive and happy at the end of the play. When we find that they are not, our faith in the efficacy of good is severely shaken, and since we have denied every value but the worldly one, we find ourselves completely bewildered. Small comfort that evil also came to a tragic end in this efficiency contest. All that means is that there are no winners, each meets a similar fate, and though we may like one more than the other, we conclude that both, like the paths of glory, lead but to the grave. We are in the world of Edmund, but he openly acknowledges his nihilism, and some of us, feeling we have discovered at the end what he knew at the beginning, find ourselves admiring his candor.

We cannot, of course, entirely escape the belief that the virtuous life is in some sense practical. I have given my reasons for concluding that *King Lear* demonstrates that it is, though not in quite the way that so many look for. The good characters in the play, most notably Cordelia, do not follow their righteous beliefs with the notion of achieving anything, or even of safeguarding anything. Tragedy is the only real test of the ultimate purity of such motivation, and in Cordelia's death we have the sublime sacrifice that triumphs over both forms of Edmundism. What this mysticism may mean to the practical mind or to the governmental philospher is a question which the play will pose as long as it continues to be performed. Cordelia can serve no Machiavellian function. Her character cannot be reduced to some portion of a text book on civics. Her rebellion is not politically inspired, nor is her loyalty. How far removed from the arena of statecraft she seems! Yet how heavy a penalty the political power pays for disregarding her pure-minded honesty and ideal love! Regardless of what form a government may take, it has no solid basis when it disregards the Cordelias of this world.

If Lear failed to see this, he is no worse than we are,

who must discover by the same painful experience the true value of what we are so willing to dismiss as "unrelated," "unessential," "pretty in its way, but trivial," and "not the stuff of which tragedy is made." We *are* Lear, as Lamb very well understood. His tragedy, while it need not be ours, need not have been his either, but is a tragedy nevertheless with which all of us can identify. Differing philosphies of government have nothing to do with it. The story relates to every historical age, neither one nor another being a barrier nor a particular kind of insight.

Once we accept Cordelia's unsullied goodness, we must accept everything it implies and let her stand as an incontrovertible chorus. No habit of thought incidental to an age can dispel what Shakespeare has taken such pains to erect, nor new definitions underestimate the power of goodness to determine what is good. When we have learned to value what Cordelia stands for, we will look with her eyes upon the father she loved and for whom she sacrificed everything. His sins and his virtues we will see as she sees them, not extenuating nor overlooking nor theorizing except as her perceptions may lead us. It is Lear's story, not hers, but never had any protagonist in Shakespeare so beautiful a light as Cordelia to shine upon him and to illumine what else were darkness.

NOTES

PREFACE

[1] J.S.H. Bransom sets forth this view in *The Tragedy of King Lear* (Basil Blackwood, Oxford, 1934, pp. 217ff), after first establishing the fact that Lear's conduct is a surprise to everyone and must therefore be explained by something that was in Lear's mind prior to the occasion. In a later work Roy W. Battenhouse (*Shakespearean Tragedy): Its Art and Its Christian Premises*, Indiana University Press, 1969, p. 277) sees the love test as an "incestuous desire for sweethearts rather than daughters."

CHAPTER I

[2] Charles Lamb, "On the Tragedies of Shakespeare," *The Complete Works and Letters of Charles Lamb* (Modern Library, New York, 1935), pp. 298-299.

[3] Harry V. Jaffa, "The Limits of Politics: An Interpretation of *King Lear,* Act I, Scene I," *American Political Science Review,* LI (1957), pp. 405–427.

It is a point in dispute as to whether Lear preferred Burgundy or the King of France to be Cordelia's husband. Jaffa feels that a marriage to Burgundy would have given Lear a tie to a potent rival of France, Britain's traditional enemy, and would therefore have been an astute political move. Futhermore, Jaffa cites the fact that when the two suitors are brought in, Lear makes his proposal first to Burgundy, as his evident choice. While I think

Jaffa's essay extremely enlightening and generally well thought out, I disagree with him on this point. To offer a daughter dowerless is hardly the way to make a political ally, particularly since Lear has already named the dowry and is now recanting. It is true that Lear speaks first to Burgundy, but only because he realizes that the offer he is about to make is a very poor one. He is much more respectful when he addresses the King of France:

> For you, great King,
> I would not from your love make such a stray,
> To match you where I hate.

[4] J.S.H. Bransom, p. 11.

[5] A.C. Bradley, *Shakespearean Tragedy* (St. Martin's Press, New York, 1965, first published London, 1904),p. 477, suggests that Kent may have been opposed to the division from the beginning. He quotes Gloucester's reflection (III, IV, 168-169):

> His daughters seek his death. Ah, that good Kent!
> He said it would be thus, poor banished man!

However, there is no need to think that Kent was referring to the original plan or that he said this some time prior to the opening of the play, and, as Bradley theorizes, fell out of royal favor as a result. When Kent is banished he is allowed five days to make provisions for his exile and on the sixth he is to turn his "hated back" upon the kingdom. During this period he has ample time to make his remark, to Gloucester or to whomever else, and if he does so he is doubtless referring to the revised plan rather than the original one. It is difficult to see how or why the daughters would seek their father's death if he were living with Cordelia in the most opulent third of the kingdom, and politically allied either to the Duke or Burgundy or to the King of France.

[6] Alfred Harbage, Introduction to *King Lear* (Pelican *Shakespeare*, Baltimore, 1964), p. 22.

[7] Contradictory explanations of Lear's folly, such as senility, long practiced arrogance, incipient madness, all attempt to find a basis that will make his action plausible, that is to say *appropriate.* Bradley (p. 282) gives a picture of the Lear that would presumably act as he does in the opening scene: ". . . a long life of absolute power, in which he has been flattered to the top of his bent, has produced in him that blindness to human limitations, and that presumptuous self-will, which in Greek tragedy we have so often seen stumbling against the altar of Nemesis. Our consciousness that the decay of old age contributes to this condition deepens our pity and our sense of human infirmity . . ." Bransom (pp. 214-215) holds similar views, mentioning Lear's irascible temperament and his tendency to make everything minister to self. He possessed, according to Bransom, "an overweening vanity and desire for adoration." These opinions are representative rather than unique.

For an excellent treatment of the qualities demanded in a king, and how they explain without excusing Lear's treatment of Cordelia and Kent, see Ivor Morris, *Shakespeare's God: The Role of Religion in the Tragedies* (George Allen & Unwin Ltd., London, 1972), pp. 342-368.

CHAPTER II

[8] I concede that the evidence for this is debatable. In the First Folio, generally admitted to be superior to the Quarto of 1608, Lear does not use the word "Speak" to Regan, though he does in the Quarto. Modern editors vary, some including the word and some omitting it. While it is true that "Speak" would render the line metrical, metrical structure is a little confused in that the following line, the beginning of Regan's reply, contains six feet. If the first of these were placed so as to be the concluding foot of the preceding line, a common arrangement in Shakespearean texts, both lines would be metrical without the word "Speak."

In the Harrison text, which I am following, I disagree with the inclusion of this word where it is addressed to Regan. Lear addresses Goneril with "Goneril, our eldest-born, speak first," since he must name the order in which the daughters are to reply. Next he turns to Regan and says, "What says our second daughter, our dearest Regan, wife to Cornwall?" Lastly he addresses Cordelia: " . . . what can you say to draw a third more opulent than your sisters?" The word "Speak" is unnecessary in these two latter instances, unless a reluctant pause were to prompt it. Regan's glibness and Cordelia's reluctance are, I believe, likely reasons for the absence of the word in the first case and its presence in the second.

[9] Elmer Edgar Stoll, *Shakespeare Studies* (Frederick Ungar, New York, 1960), p. 112.

[10] See J.S.H. Bransom (pp. 30-31).

[11] Interpreting the love test as allegory or ritual is an attempt to explain its strangeness. William Frost ("Shakespeare's Rituals and the Opening Scene of *King Lear,*"*The Hudson Review,* Vol. X, No. 4, 1957-8; reprinted in *Shakespeare's Tragedies,* ed. Laurence Lerner, Baltimore, 1964) sees everything in the opening scene from the entry of Lear as "ritualistic.". The question Lear asks his daughters is, if anything, a violation rather than a ritual. And while allegorical interpretation may be fixed upon anything that is significant or representative of broader truths, the sequence here is in a tone too low for conscious allegory.

[12] The impression is deliberately created by Shakespeare, who makes Edmund's arguments too carefully thought out to be a subconscious slip into something of which he, Shakespeare, had no knowledge but which we in the twentieth century hold to be valid. I can hardly agree with Norman N. Holland, who holds that we moderns agree with the villains rather than the good characters, since we live on this side of the seventeenth century (*The Shakespearean Imagination,* Macmillan, New York, 1964, p. 234).

[13] See A.C. Bradley.

[14] See William R. Elton, *King Lear and the Gods* (Huntington Library, San Marino, California, 1966). Though I disagree completely with Elton's conclusions, he gives a thorough and well-documented treatment of the controversies raging in Shakespeare's age between Christian thinking and what might be called the new infidelity.

[15] Leo Tolstoy, "On Shakespeare and the Drama" (tr. V. Tchertkoff. *Fortnightly Review*, LXXXVI, 1906; reprinted in *The King Lear Perplex*, .ed. Helmut Bonheim, Wadsworth, San Francisco, 1960), p. 51.

[16] H.N. Hudson, *Shakespeare: His Life, Art, and Characters* (Ginn & Company, Boston 1900), II, pp. 362-363.

CHAPTER IV

[17] An Orson Welles version of the play contained a lengthy and elaborate portrayal of drunken brawling which, if anything, surpassed even Goneril's account of what she had to endure. See also Theodore Spencer, *Shakespeare and the Nature of Man* (Macmillan, New York, 1949, first published 1942), p. 141, who accepts the "epicurism and lust" of Lear's retinue as not only true but meaningful.

[18] A.C. Bradley (p. 307).

CHAPTER V

[19] Quoted in Norman N. Holland (p. 245).

20 It seems reasonably clear, unless he speaks figuratively, that the fool is dressed in the traditional uniform of his calling. Just after he comes on stage he refers six times to his coxcomb. Later, in line 160, he alludes to himself as "the one in *motley* here."

21 I believe that the fool exemplifies something of the general pattern of pictorial representation in medieval literature, very well studied in Russell A. Fraser's *Shakespeare's Poetics: In Relation to King Lear* (Routledge and Kegan Paul, London, 1962).

CHAPTER VI

22 The persistent notions of imbecile universe and underlying chaos are a kind of groundwork for this belief. If emancipation from a "dictatorial and self-infatuated king" leads only to destruction, obviously Shakespeare was committed to the theory that only through kingship could the commonwealth survive. Post-seventeenth century history has presumably taught us otherwise, and, while there are those who make allowances for Shakespeare's inability to foresee the future, they accept his limitations with a twentieth century smile.

23 For this reason I believe it is a mistake to see Lear's madness as a kind of awakening to truths he never before realized. See Arnold Kettle, "From *Hamlet* to *Lear*," *Shakespeare in a Changing World,* ed. Arnold Kettle (International Publishers, N.Y., 1964), pp. 146-171.

CHAPTER VII

24 J.H.S. Bransom (pp. 153ff *passim*) is inclined to do this. He finds some of Cordelia's speeches "execrable poetry."

CHAPTER VIII

[25] See A.C. Bradley.

[26] William R. Elton (pp. 253-254)

[27] Wyndham Lewis, *The Lion and the Fox* (Methuen & Co., Ltd., London, 1951, first published 1927), p. 180, relies heavily on this incident to persuade us of Shakespeare's nihilism: "But the punctual arrival of Cordelia, brought in like a Christmas present, so *narquois* and so pat, cannot be anything but what it forces us at once to see it as: an expression of the poet's mockery at the vanity of human supplications, and notions of benevolent powers, of whom we are the cherished children." Lewis's reasoning, like the incident he selects, is a little too "pat" to be convincing.

[28] See Grigori Kozintsev, *Shakespeare: Time and Conscience* (Hill and Wang, New York, translated from Russian by Joyce Vining, 1966), pp. 68ff. Though Kozintsev's conclusions are not altogether despairing—he sees Lear discovering happiness and human responsibility at the end—he insists that all forms, government, offices and rank are shams through which the protagonist learns to see. The royalty of Lear was itself a sham till he was entirely divested of it and became a lowly human being. The error lies in assuming that once we have discovered evil in a particular institution we must conclude that the institution is totally evil. Surely those who remain loyal to the King remain so for some better reason than that he has discovered happiness and human responsibility at last.

[29] Jan Kott, *Shakespeare Our Contemporary*, trans. Boleslaw Taborski (Doubleday, Garden City, New York, 1966), p. 153.

[30] Bradley (p. 253) has a long footnote in which he says that "no sufficiently clear reason is supplied for Edmund's delay in attempting to save Cordelia and Lear." He suggests a number of possible reasons, but concludes that "it is surely far from satisfactory that we should be left to mere conjecture as to the cause of the delay which permits the catastrophe to take place." I

believe that Bradley is looking in the wrong place, i.e., some possible plan Edmund may have had, rather than the psychological upheaval going on his mind as a result of the sudden turn of fortune.

[31] Edmund's strange reluctance to follow Goneril's wish that he do away with her husband—

> Let her who would be rid of him devise
> His speedy taking—off

—suggests an unwillingness to cope with a formidable adversary, even by treachery, while in the same speech he determines the death of Lear and Cordelia. It may be difficult to define precisely this crack in Edmund's armor, but his self-assurance is something less than complete prior to the duel with his brother.

[32] I believe that Elton is often too quick to identify certain characters' expressions and attitudes with the neo-paganism of the time. Similarities, like passages taken out of context, must give place, and the whole play determine the meaning of all its parts.

CHAPTER IX

[33] G. Wilson Knight, *The Wheel of Fire* (Meridian Books, Cleveland and New York, 1962), pp. 187—188.

[34] William R. Elton (p. 254).

[35] Roy W. Battenhouse (p. 290)

[36] Henry Adams, *The Education of Henry Adams* (Modern Library, New York, 1931), pp. 401ff.